Running a band as a
BUSINESS

Ian Edwards, Bruce Dickinson and Phil Brookes

PC Publishing

PC Publishing
Export House
130 Vale Road
Tonbridge
Kent TN9 1SP
UK

Tel 01732 770893
Fax 01732 770268
email info@pc-publishing.co.uk
website http://www.pc-publishing.co.uk

First published 2000
© PC Publishing
An imprint of Music Technology Books Limited

ISBN 1 870775 62 7

British Library Cataloguing in Publication Data
A catalogue record for this book is available from the British Library

Printed in Great Britain by Bell and Bain, Glasgow

Contents

Dedication

Ian Edwards would like to dedicate this book to the memory of Dr John Edwards, and also to Antonella, Max and Luca with much love and thanks.

Bruce Dickinson would like to thank Janna, Edward and Rachel for all their support during the writing of this book.

Phil Brookes thanks Maggie, Colin, Natalie, Mick, Celia and Ashley.

Acknowledgments

Ian and Bruce would like to acknowledge the incredible help and support of the following people: Andrew Myers for his unerring attention to detail and unending help with the legal stuff. Kevin Nixon for his years of experience, managerial expertise and football analogies. Maria Conroy for all her help and advice regarding T-shirts and merchandise. Mike Hrano for discussing fan clubs, merchandising and telling some great (unrepeatable) stories. Patrick Haveron for all the information with regard to tribute acts, and some great (repeatable) stories.

Ian and Bruce would also like to extend their grateful thanks to all at Future Publishing for their support and help with the photographs. In particular they would like to thank Sarah Clark, Gavin Roberts, Simon Dodd, Rob Scott, James Cumpsty, Richard Ecclestone and Justin Scobie.

Finally the authors would like to extend their gratitude to Simon Haisman for giving his permission for the reproduction of the photographs in this book.

About the authors

*I*an Edwards has spent much of his life playing in bands, studying music and the music industry, and has set up his own record label. He received a First Class BA (Hons) Degree in World Music and History and currently works as the Publicity & Promotions Officer at ACM.

Bruce Dickinson has had eleven top forty hits and a number one album with his band Little Angels. He has toured with Van Halen, Aerosmith, Bon Jovi, ZZ Top and Bryan Adams. Bruce is currently School Manager at ACM where he lectures on the music business and teaches guitar.

Phil Brookes is a qualified classical and electric guitar player and has worked closely with the music industry and education combining an entrepreneurial flair with intense vision for the future of rock and popular music education. Phil Brookes is owner and Director of The Academy of Contemporary Music – Europe's leading school for rock and pop musicians.

Taking care of business

Welcome to the music business – arguably the most exciting and competitive industry in the world. There's a lot of money and great times to be had for those artists who get it right – and pain, misery, poverty and broken dreams for those who don't. Never underestimate how vicious the music business can be. Bruce Dickinson, one of the authors of this book, recalls:

> 'When I was 16 years old my band and all the other musicians in our town were absolutely convinced beyond a shadow of a doubt that we were going to be famous. Fifteen years later with hindsight I can look back and see that only a tiny, tiny percentage of us got through and had any kind of success in the business. Some of those guys we left behind are now in their mid 30's and playing music hopelessly out of date but still convinced that one day they will still be a big star.'

Today there are even more bands, more great players, more songs to be heard and ultimately of course, more losers to get bitter and twisted in their old age when fickle fame and fortune pass them by. That's the bad news – the good news is that yes, some of those artists will be successful, and the reasons behind that success will be less to do with luck, and more to do with factors that the artist can control than popular belief might suggest. Successful musicians are nearly always incredibly motivated, focused people with important ideas to communicate and something to say. These characters cut through the bullshit and often have explosively successful careers.

Living the rock 'n' roll dream – The Wildhearts

Our first important lesson is to realise that in music, as in life, nobody gets anything for nothing. On hearing a track on the radio that is not immediately understood or identified with, most inexperienced artist's reaction is to ignore it, usually with a dismissive 'That's crap!' This could be a big mistake. Every artist in the Top 40 is there for a reason and is filling some kind of niche. Smart young musicians learn from every possible source. A record whose appeal you don't understand deserves more attention and more analysis, not less, than a track you like immediately.

It is often forgotten by musicians that music is a form of communication, and as a performer if you can get into the minds of your audience and understand why they listen to, and relate to, certain songs you will have begun your transition from bedroom dreamer to true artist. This isn't all about you and what you want – yes you do want fame, money, the chance to play music for a living but you're going to have to give of yourself in return. So let's get started with the single most important stage in your success story:

Getting it together

Whether you're a credible indie guitar outfit or the cheesiest cover band on the planet it doesn't matter. It's vital to be *something* – to be defined. Be the cleverest, be the dumbest, the sexiest, the nerdiest, the hardest. Get the idea?

Remember late 80's US pop metal act, Motley Crue? They were a multimillion-selling band with gold and platinum discs all round the world. Why? They weren't the most accomplished musicians in the world – although they had a great rhythm section and the records sounded huge, courtesy of Bob Rocks' state of the art late

80's production. What really made the band stand out was their world class stupidity. They weren't the cleverest but they were the dumbest! If you were 14 and liked metal, a hooky chorus, lyrics about sex, drugs and rock 'n roll, you didn't have to look any further than Motley Crue. They worked on the same basic formula as tens of thousands of other bands, but took it further becoming (literally) comic book characters. Because they were so well defined they became the world's No. 1 dumb pop metal band and we loved them for it! More importantly, we bought their records in millions.

The brilliantly stupid Motley Crue

Let's take a more up to date example with Cornershop and their number 1 track 'Brimful of Asha'. The ironic name coupled with the authentic Indian instruments, scales and hip drums and bass was perfectly timed when the breezy appeal of Brit Pop was starting to wear thin. The vibe was perfect and each track on their album reinforced the overall direction. Imagine if Cornershop's second single had featured a hard techno production style. It would have blown the whole vibe overnight. Sounds ridiculous? Yes, but most demo tapes cover too many styles. All half-decent bands can have a crack at a few styles (a reggae track here, a progressive bit of jazz-fusion here, a bit of sampling, etc, etc). But great artists have a vision and direction and can communicate that vision in every bar of music, every photograph and every lyric.

For this reason it didn't really matter which label Lenny Kravitz signed to in the mid 80's, because that artist was onto something and was going to get through somehow. Kravitz didn't want to recreate the late 60's, he just wanted to bring back the spirit of those times. Retro sounds are commonplace now but then, when everyone was constructing careful sonic pictures in the studio and taking four days to get the right high hat sound, Kravitz's Warm Analogue one take performances complete with buzz's, glitches and mistakes were a sonic revelation. And to top it all, this amazingly photogenic guy with the wild hair was wearing flares while we were all trying to pull on the skinniest black stretchy jeans we could get. With a vibe and direction as strong as that, Lenny was going to get his message heard somehow. It just happened to be A&M records that were the medium for Kravitz to communicate his vision.

So decide on the direction for your act. Firstly, are you a cabaret type of outfit gigging to make money or are you a serious original band aiming for a long term career and international hit records? Sounds like an obvious point, doesn't it? But if you're mixing cover versions with original songs you've got to go one way or the other. Function audiences don't want to hear your latest self-penned masterpiece and you'll lose all your credibility with NME when you launch into 'I Will Survive' by Gloria Gaynor.

What's in a name?

We can go two ways with the name, either specific or non-specific. A specific name lets the audience know what they're in for before even a bar of music is heard. 'Boyzone' for example – you can bet you're going to get four or five young, good-looking lads who can dance and get the girlies going with their poppy, commercial hits. Sure enough, that's what we get! Take the name 'Metallica' – which evokes mental pictures of long hair, massive crunchy riffs and stadium metal. No surprises there when we investigate further and find that music and the look of the act are exactly as we imagined. The name epitomises the vibe of the act in both cases. The downside of a specific name is that, although it is immensely helpful for a fledgling outfit who need the added impetus of a movement to kick start their career, it can, and will, be a handicap to an established band wishing to develop and broaden their musical horizons. It's going to be difficult to be in Boyzone when you're 35 years of age and Metallica are always going to be filed under Heavy Metal in HMV!

So our indie band (who could be called 'The Shoe Gazers' – if they wanted to be specific) decide 'No – we want to have a new non-specific name to enable us to grow as our careers progress like REM, UB40, U2 or even The Stone Roses'. It's worth remembering that numbers and letters make vague-sounding but epic names. So The Shoe Gazers change their name to 'The B51's' and sacrifice short term advantages for a gamble on long term success.

If your act is a cabaret style money making venture it is wise to remember this simple equation: more cheese = more money. Therefore the cheesier the name the more potential earning power of the act. Patrick Haveron from the UK's largest tribute band agency 'Psycho Management' comments 'It's all about getting a good pun. When I'm selling an act into a venue I can always get

Utter Madness – getting in on the act with a well defined tribute band name.

more money on a band with a great name like 'No Way Sis' (Oasis tribute band), 'AC Seedy' (AC/DC), 'Pretend Pretenders', 'Closet Queen' and 'Counterfeit Stones'. Of course it's not cool. In fact the reason I can get gigs on the university circuit is because these bands are so uncool they transcend that dividing line and actually become credible to a sophisticated audience who can see the irony'.

So the moral of the story so far is, firstly, decide on your direction. Be able to articulate what you do in a simple phrase. If no words exist to describe your 'new' sound, invent a label – 'acid jazz' didn't exist until somebody came up with a great spin on some old phrases. If you're having difficulty describing the sound in your head, ask yourself these questions:

1 Who would my band want to support on tour?
2 Who would be the best producer for the band?
3 Which section of the public would be the most likely market for the act?

If you can say with certainty – 'my band would like to support Skunk Anansie, be produced by Steve Harris (Bluetones, Kula Shaker) and sell records to the young politically aware rock and indie crowds', then you've made significant progress in defining the direction in your own mind. And, if you're well defined in your own mind, you then have much more chance of communicating your vision to others – be they fans or A&R men.

Now that you know where you're going, it's time to choose, replace, sack and hire band members to create the ultimate success machine!

Wanna be in my gang?

Many of the most successful bands in the world were started in the same way; key members of the band coming together as kids and growing up with a shared dream to be just like their heroes on Top Of The Pops. The seeds of super-stardom are sown long before a guitar or drumstick is even picked up, and this relationship can produce some of the most enduring and productive partnerships in music. The problem from our point of view is that the whole business is rather chancy. Imagine the odds against two talents as rare as Lennon and McCartney finding each other in childhood. Compound that with the chances of any two random artists actually functioning effectively as a team and we begin to realise that, although fate will throw up great bands by coincidence every now and then, the statistical likelihood of finding yourself in another U2 or Beatles is remote. However, the dream does happen for some bands: Blur, Shed Seven and Orbital all managed to realise their

Paul Banks – had a band
even before he had a guitar!

childhood dreams through their music. Paul Banks, ex guitarist
with Shed Seven, tells us the history behind the band:

> 'It started when I was 11. I met Rick (Whitter, vocals) and we
> were both into music. He had stacks of records, and we formed a
> band before I even had a guitar! We listened to stuff like Frankie
> Goes To Hollywood – we were too young for The Smiths. It was
> obvious chart stuff, U2, things like that. Dad bought me a guitar
> and I taught myself to play and we just used to sit and write crap
> songs together.'

One of the authors of this book, Bruce Dickinson, signed a major
recording contract and went on to enjoy a run of hit records in the
early'90s with a band that had started out with a bunch of school
friends playing gigs at school and at the local scout hut. He
remembers:

> 'When we first started out at 16 years old we truly believed that
> we were the best band on the planet. We weren't, obviously, but
> although we couldn't really play or write songs we did have enor-
> mous self-belief and determination to succeed. Because we were
> all friends we built each other up and created a world of our own
> where we were already rock stars in our own minds. The belief
> was so strong it became a self-fulfilling prophecy and other peo-
> ple started to believe it too. I don't know if you could ever get
> that energy in the same way in a band that didn't grow up
> together.'

So this approach can be, and is, successful, but it is by no means
the only way. Imagine you and your mates have decided to invest
your time and hard earned pocket money in some instruments,
written half a dozen songs of dubious quality and believe that your
band is just about to hit the 'big time'. What happens? The bass

player finds a girl friend and is no longer interested in music and the drummer decides to go to college because his mum and dad have put the thumb-screws on. Never fear, all is not lost. In fact the disappearing band members have done you a large favour early on in your career as you will need all your powers of determination to make it in this industry, and you cannot afford to carry any passengers who are just in it for the ride.

Limiting factors

For a band to reach its full potential it is important to identify anything that might be a 'limiting factor' within that act. A limiting factor can be defined as anything that will prevent you from achieving your full potential. Remember that your band is only as strong as the weakest link. We know, from our earlier discussions, that how well defined our project is will be one of our 'limiting factors'. Having decided what and who we are, who's going to be into what we do and what we're going to call ourselves, we should now turn are attention to the music and ask ourselves the simple question 'is it any good?'

1 Song writing

It is a fact that most bands significantly overestimate the standard of their song writing and therefore never reach anything near their full potential simply because they do not research and analyse modern and classic material and great recordings. One of the problems that we have already encountered as musicians is that family and friends are quick to pronounce any old demo as a masterpiece. Comments like 'That's brilliant that is, much better than all that rubbish on Top of the Pops' are well meant, but not helpful to the smart writer trying to set his standards at the highest level.

Sheryl Crow – an artist with some great tunes. How do yours measure up?

Let us examine the type of tracks that we are going to need to get our careers off the ground. Most artists' careers are dependent on certain 'turning point' or career breaking recordings. These are the songs which convince the fans to buy the demo, the A&R guys to sign the band, the radio to play the single and punters in their thousands to sing along with the song all over the world. We're talking about hits. Recordings that change lives – not least the lives of the talented individuals who wrote them. So it's no good comparing your demo with an average album track of your favourite artist, because your work needs to have the substance and the weight of those big hits.

Successful artists without exception spend a huge amount of time researching and analysing material. Jools Holland calls the process 'Trawling'. Trawling for licks, chord sequences, melodic and lyrical ideas, sounds, production tricks, drum grooves, cool fills, bass lines etc etc. Serious writers know that learning their craft well takes work, but that's okay because we love music anyway and most of us are fascinated by what makes it tick. Perhaps we should really be looking at what makes *us* tick. What are the triggers that make us respond to certain pieces in certain ways? Bruce Dickinson recalled observing the reaction of a group of young children on hearing Puff Daddy's 'Come with Me', the theme from the film Godzilla.

> 'The kids went mental and they were running around everywhere pretending to be Godzilla and making monster noises. My wife said that that must be the best monster music ever written to make those little kids react like that. It got me thinking why does that track make you feel that way? Those powerful, Bonham-style drums and that evil augmented riff really do the job.
>
> At the Academy we studied the recording and the students learned that one way of achieving power on a track was to drag the drums back behind the beat. Of course we learned a whole lot more than that just from one track. My point is this: when music makes you feel a certain way try and work out why. Good writers and performers know all the emotional buttons to press – a minor chord for example is going to sound sad, a major chord will probably sound happy. These are obvious examples, but imagine how quickly a musician will improve if they are constantly analysing a broad range of quality material every day absorbing the language of music and the skills of communication through the best music of the past and present.'

So we know that as well as great band members we need world-beating songs. We need our own 'career breaking' tracks. It's worth noting that many bands fall down on the quality of their subject matter. The Academy of Contemporary Music receives demo tapes through the post every day. Very few lyricists have something of substance to say. Professional song writer, arranger, producer and consultant at The Academy, Jimmy D, of The Younger Younger 28's commented:

> 'Pop lyric writing is a very misunderstood art form. Any one can churn out pseudo intellectual 6th form gibberish, but the real issue is what are you talking about? Have you got something to say that I will be interested in? The language you use can be simple or complex in style it really doesn't matter. What is a problem is a writer who tries to disguise the lack of an idea in his lyric with flowery imagery. Ideas come from living life, so it's more difficult for a very young artist to have enough life experience to come up with subject matter to compete with a guy like, say, Jarvis Cocker or Joe Northern who's been through drugs, depression, relationships and all the rest of it.
>
> The young writers, who are any good, are out there living life at a very fast pace, and you tend to find that the 'eternal support bands' destined never to get anywhere ain't writing about strong ideas, simply because nothing much is going on in their lives.'

So, there we have it – a successful band will need the ability to write definitive hit records, to possess strong musical content, i.e. to be able to play or programme well enough to ensure the quality of the recording, and produce strong subject matter.

> **TIP**
>
> Somebody within every band needs to be able to analyse hit records, and conclude why those records were or are successful. Remember to focus on those big career-breaking tracks.

2 Commercial viability

Many musicians refuse to consider the question of whether their music is relevant to the present music scene, even regarding the concept of commercialising their product as immoral. Ironically it is often these same individuals who expect to get a recording contract, fame and wealth entirely on their own terms. Unfortunately they are likely to be disappointed.

One of the functions of popular music is to represent the time that it is created in, providing a soundtrack to history as it happens. What better way to evoke the feeling of the conflict in Vietnam than a Hendrix track from the same time? Early 80's synth pop like Yazoo and Depeche Mode will always remind the thirty-something generation of their formative teenage years. So it falls to you, as an artist of today, to create the music of today. That's your role and if you're a bit out of date either sonically or visually, then get worried. Do something about it!

The Music Business is a fashion based industry and there are two ways you can go at this point:

1 Be right on top of current trends
2 Set the pace – invent your look and sound and let the pack follow you.

Some people have got it and some ain't. Bruce recalls:

'When I was in a band I wasn't very good at being a rock star. I'd look at Slash or David Bowie and think 'Yeah – they know what they're doing' but I could never get it to work for me. I'd go into a shop and see a row of shirts and not know which one would look cool and which one would look stupid. Mark Richardson (drummer – now with Skunk Anansie) on the other hand would always get it right. If he had his haircut it would be the business and if he bought shades they would be mean. Me, I'd buy a pair and they would look wonky and the lens would fall out.

At the Academy we often send students for auditions and sometimes we get a great musician who's a bit square. It can be difficult to place those players because you can't just make someone cool – it's either ingrained already or it's going to take serious work. One thing I have noticed is that the students who do get the gigs read the right fashion and music magazines, they watch current films, go to hip clubs and gigs, party and network a lot and generally live the life. If you're immersed in popular culture you're going to develop a sense of what is cool without trying.'

Most of us can recognise cool and uncool looks and sounds, but fall down when it comes to having the objectivity and the imagination to create a vibe ourselves. So try following some simple keys to street credibility:

TIP

Put as much effort into your image as your music – you want to look good on MTV don't you?

1 Be objective and hard on yourselves. If the bass player wears a shell suit with his T shirt tucked in and his tracky bottoms pulled right up it might be a very convincing anti-fashion statement – on the other hand it might just be plain uncool. You know the difference.
2 Detail is important. Liam Gallagher's zipped up hooded top look launched a million copyists. Understatement is an art form in itself.
3 If you aren't a natural born fashion guru don't be afraid to ask for help. If one of your mates is consistently well turned out, get him to help you choose your kit.
4 Find labels, which you like and stick to them. These designers are pros – if you liked surf gear a couple of years ago then Stussey or No Fear would have done all the work for you. You know it's cool. You know it'll all go together. How can you go wrong?
5 Hair colour and cut is so important in music. Again get advice. Don't be afraid to experiment with dyes, bleach, bunches, plaits and accessories. Look at what Lisa Stansfield and Bjork managed to achieve with a little thought and imagination.

6 Read plenty of magazines, not just the music publications. Find your own reference points that are appropriate to where you and your music are coming from.

Hours in front of the mirror – Shane McGowan works on his image
Pic courtesy Andy Catlin

3 Band chemistry

Why is it that some of the greatest bands in the world are made up of players and singers of only average ability? Why is it that countless 'Supergroups', carefully constructed from the most talented artists from all over the world, have so often failed to live up to expectations and have delivered limp performances and recordings? More than anything else the band's potential depends on how efficiently the individual members function as a team. The complex physiology of who does what, and their motives for doing it, creates working environments that stimulate some artists and repress others. Nearly all bands have something great about them; a talented member, a good player or good songwriter but few working relationships allow the true talent in the band to develop unhindered.

Let us examine the reasons why artists wish to perform. Ask a roomful of musicians why they play, write songs and make records and most will reply 'Because I love music'. True enough, but they could love music and get just as much enjoyment out of composing and playing for their own sakes in their bedrooms. If the truth were told most musicians in bands are driven by the need to perform, the need to be recognised. The greater the need the more intense the drive the artist will have to perform and write. When we consider that an individual's need for recognition usually stems from deep-rooted insecurity, we quickly appreciate why a band's chemistry can be such a volatile and unstable affair. In any other business it would be madness to assemble a team of temperamental, insecure and emotionally unstable personalities together and expect them to work as a unit!

Bruce Dickinson remembers the stresses and strains of working in an intensive team situation and commented:

'If you've got five people working together there's always somebody being a pain in the arse at any one time. It can get very wearing and tempers do fray. It's difficult being a band member because your career depends on other people having some degree of common sense. Unfortunately those most talented creatively are often the least practical. Most people who play in an ambitious band will identify with me when I say that the frustration of dealing with musicians and day to day practicalities together can be unbearable. However the only thing that really matters is the music. It's much better to be in an outfit that constantly argue like cat and dog if you make great records, than play in a band with your best friends producing average material.'

So how do we make sure that the team working practices in a band allow the band to reach its creative potential? Well there are certain character types and stereotypes that really do exist. Recognising and understanding what drives your colleagues can make your working practices more pleasant and more productive.

Vocalists, for example, are the focus of attention in the band and it is not surprising that it is here that we find the individuals with the greatest need for recognition. Eddie Van Halen refers to a condition called 'LSD' or Lead Singer Disease when he describes the friction he inevitably seemed to experience with vocalists in Van Halen. It can help you to deal with difficult and temperamental band members if you rationalise that the very things that make the

Dodgy – great songwriting teams don't necessarily always get on personally as individuals.

individuals hard to work with are the characteristics that make them a good performer. The bigger the ego and insecurity the more that individual requires recognition. They don't feel good within themselves and so they need to be 'told' by an adoring crowd, a hit record, or a fan asking for an autograph that they are liked and accepted. Truly great artists are often subject to extreme mood swings depression and problems with drink and drugs. Eric Clapton said, when talking about Jimi Hendrix, 'when you visit those dark places you can't take anybody with you'. If the performer is good enough we, and the rest of the world, will forgive incredible excess of bad behaviour. However, there are limits ...

The Academy of Contemporary Music recently hosted a masterclass by one of rock's legendary 'difficult characters': guitar hero Yngwie Malmsteen. Yngwie, who arrived two hours late, had several tantrums over: hairspray (lack of), mirror (size of), dressing room (location of) and the fact that too many of the audience were 'looking at him'. Yngwie delivered a stunning performance, which lasted 20 minutes, before refusing to sign autographs and leaving. Fans had paid to see a two-hour show. Students were left to come to their own conclusions as to why Yngwie's band line up changed every few months, and why Yngwie's career had taken such a different path from that of some of his more successful guitar shredding contemporaries.

From our point of view the standard of our band members' behaviour, and how easy they are to get along with is not perhaps as important as the quality of the music we produce. It probably was hard work being in The Who, living with the tension between Daltrey and Townshend and the wild antics of Keith Moon. Hard work or not the chemistry worked and between them they produced some of the most important works in popular music. Let me give you two examples of bands with the same levels of ability. One band (A) produces music well beyond the individual abilities of the members, and the other (B) whose music sadly fails to live up to the obvious potential of the act.

Band A

Band A has two main songwriters. There is a strong element of competition between the pair, which results in the writing standards being driven higher and higher as each composer tries to write a better song than his colleague. One of the writers is an outstanding melody writer but can tend to lapse into sentimentality and banality if left unchecked. The other writer is a hardened cynic, deeply incisive but can tend towards self-indulgence. The combination of the two characters together produces the strongest material. The other band members are less intense and contribute to the project by preventing the inevitable clashes of ego from getting out of hand, adding arrangement and instrumentation skills and identifying the strongest material.

TIP

*B*eing in a great team that is pushing the individual members to the absolute brink of their creative potential is rarely comfortable – no pain no gain!

Band B

Band B also has two main songwriters. One of the songwriters is a world class talent but not assertive or confident. The second writer has only average ability but is determined to get his own material through whatever the cost and lacks the objectivity to make accurate assessments of the quality of his work. The other two members recognise the problem but lack the strength of character to address it. Many bands have one dominant character who calls the shots and controls the decision making process within the unit. This can be a great way of working if the artist has a strong vision and the practical skills to realise that vision. One of the authors toured with Bon Jovi and observed:

> 'Jon was without question the absolute leader of the band. He made the decisions and the other guys went with that. In the past it had caused conflict in the group and at one stage both Jon and Ritchie (Sambora – guitarist) released solo records. Jon had a huge hit all over the world with 'Blaze of Glory', and Ritchie, to cut along story short, didn't. I think that really enforced the pecking order and enabled Jon to take control. He's sharp as a razor and really knows where he's going with that band so it does make sense to keep your trap shut and ears open in that situation. All those musicians were onto a good thing courtesy of Jon's talent and brains but it was probably only in the latter stages of their career that they came to terms with that.'

The moral of the tale is if you're lucky enough to find a Lenny Kravitz, Bon Jovi or a Madonna, realise that artists of this calibre are probably going to be successful with or without you. It's not all plain sailing however – the trouble with being a member of an act with a particularly dominant character who calls the shots, is that your career is in the hands of another person. This can be fine as long as the dominant member has 'vision', the practical skills to realise that vision and some degree of common sense or streetwise suss. Bands fall down when dominant personalities take over aspects of the band's development to the detriment of the potential of the act. Bruce Dickinson remembers this being a problem in his old band Little Angels:

> 'In the early days of our band we all wrote the songs together. There was a lot of individual talent in the band, particularly my brother Jimmy and Toby the singer. For one reason and another we never could combine what Jimmy had – a great sense of groove, arrangement and an instinctive feel for a cool vibe – with Toby's abilities as a singer songwriter. In hindsight the fact that Jimmy couldn't get his ideas through and the fact that Toby wasn't perhaps as open to creative input from other band members as he could have been, meant that the band never fully realised its potential.'

Crispian Mills of Kula Shaker who sold two million copies all over the world with their debut album 'K'

A dominant or lead member who feels a little too in control of the band's future, without understanding that it is not just them who are forging the band's success and future potential success, can in extreme cases do irreparable damage to the unit.

A classic example of this in recent times is the Kula Shaker story. Signed to Kevin Nixon Management for a two album deal, Kula Shaker went from scratch to selling two million copies all over the world with their debut album 'K'. They never seemed to be off the radio or the television. Kula Shaker was a great band. They were also lucky enough to have one of the best managers in the business, Kevin Nixon, working on their project. Nixon, a tough and seasoned professional, controlled the career path of the band and did his best to temper the wilder excesses of Crispian Mill's outspoken views. Crispian found this hard to cope with and desperately wanted to take full control of the band whatever the cost. Finding that in a direct battle of wills he couldn't compete with Nixon, Crispian decided to sack his manager. Picture the scene – a band coming from the garage to a two million selling album and then wanting to sack the management that had helped put them there.

Self destruction comes in many forms, not just drink and drugs. Fame, financial success, records in the charts, public adulation, awards and being in the most happening band of the time just wasn't enough for Crispian. Incredible as it seems, he was prepared to risk losing everything to gain control.

Kula Shaker had signed for a two album commitment on their management contract, and so a bitter legal battle ensued which was finally settled out of court in Nixon's favour. Very much in Nixon's favour. Kula Shaker, now considerably out of pocket, had gone from the band most likely to break America to the band who were rapidly being forgotten. They desperately needed to pull something

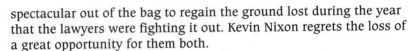

spectacular out of the bag to regain the ground lost during the year that the lawyers were fighting it out. Kevin Nixon regrets the loss of a great opportunity for them both.

> 'The realistic chance to take an act from two million sales to five million comes perhaps once every ten years. To lose that chance is ... frustrating for everyone involved.'

For every star who gets through, scores fall at the final fence – making unbelievably bad decisions and taking bad advice at crucial points in their careers.

4 Subject matters

Most people are attracted to music that they like the sound of, but when it comes to buying a record your average punter will go for a band or a track that they feel some affinity with. They either identify with the music and vibe, or something about the act gives the listener an identity that they can claim for their own. It is no coincidence that young people searching for their place as adults in the world are the most passionate consumers of popular music. The bands represent not just an attractive noise to listen to, but a role model and a lifestyle statement. An 18 year-old will more readily identify with a 20 year-old artist than a 40 year-old. How many times have you heard a track that you really like on the radio but not actually bought the piece, two or three times a week perhaps? What is it that actually triggers the impulse to own a recording, because, let's face it, we can listen to as much great music as we like just by listening to the radio?

The records that you do buy are the one's that tend to represent you, that stand for what you think and believe in either lyrically, musically or sonically. That is why bands that are well defined are more likely to break through. If you look historically at bands that are successful, that reach a lot of people, their lyric writing has usually been a vital component to their success. Bands that do not get through tend to be lyrically directionless and wishy-washy.

We deal with a large number of young bands at the Academy and one of the first things we address is their lyrical content. Many young bands when asked what a particular song is about are unsure, because generally it is not really about anything or it is just a half idea. The whole key to success as a young artist is to have the necessary life experience in a few short years to actually write about subjects that really move other people. If your songwriter's reading consists of a couple of Stephen King books a year then his or her lyrics are not likely to be particularly heavyweight or well informed.

But we are talking about rock 'n' roll here and we can consider

The Beastie Boys to be brilliant lyricists, yet they will never be Ernest Hemingway. They write material that millions of us identify with. 'Fight for your Right to Party' is not a 'serious' lyric – but it's a seriously good lyric. If there's a character in your band with something to say that they feel very passionate about then maybe other people will too. If you're 18 years old and feel sympathy with Skin from Skunk Anansie's biting political broadsides, or Rage Against The Machine's attacks against the American Dream, then you'll probably want to 'own' those statements by buying the record.

Ultimately the achievement of good band chemistry involves functioning effectively as a team, with a balance that incorporates the dominant and the less dominant personalities within that team to ensure it functions efficiently. Remember, too many dominant personalities can lead to a band war and self destruction, and it is not always necessary for the team to actually get on particularly well as long as the collective goals are the same. It doesn't matter if one member is a tosser as long as he is a tosser and you can still get the job done!

Guitar and lager – (never mind the load of old bollocks)

Steve Jones of the Sex Pistols – good song titles shame about the tracky bottoms

The one thing that really matters is the end result, the music. And that means getting what is inherently in the band out musically, getting it recorded and placed onto disc or tape. With a great product, a hot image and the right attitude you stand a fighting chance of getting in to one of the most exciting and sought after industries in the world. Of course you may find that after all your best efforts you cannot get your band members up to scratch. Maybe they don't share your high standards, and rather than spend time fighting a losing battle you decide to quit the band and audition yourself to the top.

Auditions – how to organise them and how to pass them

The first thing to think about when you are either looking to audition other musicians for your band, or to audition for bands yourself, is where to look. This is the easy bit because nearly all publications that are linked with the music business carry audition listings in the classified sections at the back of the publication. *The Stage, Melody Maker, Guitarist, Total Guitar,* etc. all carry ads every month. If you are seriously looking to join a band or recruit other members then start there, and also consider subscribing to *Music Week* to find out what's going on in the business.

Most of the auditions ads are taken out by dodgy support bands and bedroom dreamers, but in amongst the dogs will be a few big bands and a few amazing up and coming acts. Even if it takes 20 auditions to get yourself in a decent band at least by the time you get your shot at a great gig you're going to be pretty hot at actually doing auditions! It may sound obvious but the music business in the UK is based in London, and the odds of being successful in the capital when you're punting for a new band are greater, simply because there are more acts to choose from.

So as an individual musician out in the marketplace we now face two separate challenges: to get a quality audition and to make the most of that opportunity and actually pass it! Here's the good news – if 400 musicians are going for a particular audition there will probably be only 5 of them that are not going to make basic mistakes. If we can analyse what the basic mistakes are and not fall into those traps, then when you go for your next audition you will be seriously narrowing the odds of getting the gig in your favour.

To impress or not to impress

Most people go into an audition situation wanting to impress the person or people who are holding the audition, they are anxious about coming across as being a really great player or singer and so tend to try too hard. In nearly any musical situation, whether it is a cabaret-style act, a tribute band, or whether it is a rock or pop outfit at a high level, the people holding the audition will be looking for good quality playing, and a player who knows how to play in an appropriate manner. This usually means simple parts played incredibly well, and knowing when you can rip it up. This fine balance of craftsmanship, taste and keeping your playing or singing exciting is an art form all in itself.

If we look at drums as an example, the first drummer that enters the audition room who can lay down a straight groove with or without a click, hit the drums hard and get an appropriate and consistent 'sound', who can be totally in time and use his fills tastefully ensuring they are placed for maximum effect, will almost certainly get the gig. Mark Richardson explained how he got the gig with multi-platinum rock band Skunk Anansie at a recent Academy of Contemporary Music masterclass.

'Well to tell the truth it all started at a party. I was pissed and I bumped into Skin (lead singer) I'd seen the band play at Nottingham Rock City and thought they were amazing, but I didn't rate the drummer. The whole band was giving it everything at this gig but the drums were too tickly and didn't have enough bollocks. I new I could do that job and because I was pissed I said, well slurred, to Skin 'You lot are brilliant but you're drummer's shit. You should give the gig to me' To my surprise she replied ' We're changing drummers actually, come for an audition.'

So I turned up for the audition. Of course this was in the cold light of day and I'd lost that confidence you get when you're pissed out of your tree. But I'd done enough gigs and recording to know that what works best in most situations is simple, solid, consistent playing. So I concentrated on getting a good feel and gave it everything I had. The other players at the audition made it easy for me by fiddling around – loads of toms, fills and extra bass drums. Nothing destroys a groove faster than the wrong bass drum part. My advice to anyone going for a big audition is to hold off on your flashy stuff. Assert yourself by showing you are an experienced professional. Pros tend to sketch out the track simply. Concentrate on the groove and the feel but don't bin the excitement. The key word is control. I really belt the kit but I don't speed up when I hit hard. Most players get nervous or

Mark Richardson from Skunk Anansie – who says the music business is a lottery?

excited and their playing gets real pushy and as a result it sounds like a little kid messing about.

I'm not just talking about drums – a solid guitarist will always be more use in a band than a bedroom widdler who can't hold it down. It's interesting that if you ask most guitarists to play something exciting they'll play something really technical. That may be exciting to them because they play guitar and they know it's hard to do. It isn't exciting to me, I'm not a guitar player – I get off on a great riff or someone who looks great and plays three chords like they mean it. I just turned that thinking around and thought what is exciting and useful drumming to a guitarist, singer or a guy in the crowd at a gig.'

So the first thing to do when it's your turn in the hot seat, and your future depends on how you perform in the next ten minutes, is to ask 'what do these guys want from me?' and *listen* to the answer. Then take a few seconds to just think about it. Then 'sketch out' the piece of music as simply as possible. If you are playing guitar then just play the chords, play them simply and get the feel of the piece. Once it feels good you can stretch yourself. Try not to be boring or under play, but make sure you choose your moment to put in that killer lick or phrase to demonstrate that you are capable of a combination of control and taste; think about what you are going to do and when you are going to do it. If you are sent a tape of the music before the audition then make sure that you learn it! This preparation is absolutely essential. We have a saying at the Academy of Contemporary Music – don't practise something until you can play it right, practise it until you can't play it wrong.There is a vast difference between these two approaches. Just because you can play something in your bedroom does not mean that you will be able to cut it in an unusual room, surrounded by strangers and possibly using a strange amp, drum kit or vocal PA. You must be confident that you could play that piece of music under any circumstances.

TIP

*D*on't practise something until you can play it **right**, practise it until you **can't** play it wrong.

Nervous? You will be

One simple way of helping to ease tension within yourself is to ensure that you do not arrive late. Allow plenty of time to get to the audition, to set up any equipment, make sure you are in tune and maybe even practise a few scales to warm up. However, whatever you do to prepare yourself, the chances are that you will be nervous. Even the most well known professional musicians can get nervous in auditions so do not let it overwhelm you. There are many well-documented ways to help people come to terms with nerves, deep breathing exercises for example, but one very simple trick is to just accept that you are nervous. Be 'nervous' – everyone else will be, and that while you may feel that you will not be able to play or sing to your optimum ability, neither will they.

Auditions are like all things in life, you need to practise them to gain knowledge and understanding. So if you have applied for an audition with a band and they send you a tape and photo of themselves that is not really the style that you are looking for, learn the songs and go to the audition anyway. It is good practice, it will help with your discipline and experience of these situations, and next time you attend an audition for a band that you do really like, you will be better prepared and far less apprehensive.

Attitude problems

Many a great musician has never got or held down a big gig, because he is difficult to work with. If a band get a sniff of the fact that an individual may be a 'pain in the arse' in the audition then that player ain't going to get the gig. One of the authors remembers auditioning drummers for a band on a major label and being surprised at how few players had an understanding of profession-alism even at that level.

'There were stacks and stacks of drummers turning up for the gig and it meant that we didn't have time to spend ages on the audi-tion, in fact each guy only got about five minutes unless we real-ly liked them. Even in that short space of time it's surprising how easy it is to spot the musicians with the attitude problems and weed them out. One bloke even turned up with a roadie, he prob-ably thought that this would make him look like a real pro. Anyone who whined about anything was instantly crossed off the list. We were using an old crappy kit deliberately to see who could cope with difficult situations and who couldn't. It was amazing seeing the gulf between the experienced players who just sat down and did the job, and all the others who spent ages adjusting stands and changing bass drum pedals, bitching and moaning.

When you've done a few auditions you do see patterns, and those players who create a fuss are usually insecure about their skills and need everything to be perfect before they can play well. Of course what we were looking for was a guy who could hack it in any situation. Can you imagine opening a big festival with no soundcheck and ten minutes to get the gear onstage with one of those whingey insecure types in the band?'

Professionalism means not making a fuss. If you arrive at the audition and the equipment they have provided is not to your liking, do not make excuses beforehand or say that you can't play through that sort of amp. If you can deal with any situation without making a fuss and make the job of the people holding the audition easier not harder, then you are another step closer to landing the gig. If you also find that you can get on with them socially as well as professionally then you are 50 per cent home and dry. Make sure you continue your professional attitude through to the end of the audition, do not hang around asking whether you got the gig or making a pest of yourself. If you got the gig then you will hear about it in the next few days. There is nothing wrong with following up the audition with a phone call a few days later however as it is quite possible that the band, in typical rock 'n roll fashion, have lost your phone number. If you did not get the job this time you may have come really close, so do not worry, there is always next time.

It is worth bearing in mind that in an audition situation you will need to be 'well-rounded'. There is no point being that cool, tasty player who has learned the tape and is ready to impress if you turn up wearing slacks, a cardigan and tartan slippers! (unless you're going for the Val Doonican gig). Rock 'n roll and the music business is fashion based so if you have the right sunglasses and the right haircut and you can play and you don't make too much of a tool of yourself – then the gig is almost certainly yours.

Golden rules

1 Don't be late and never make a fuss or make excuses
2 Don't try to be a 'big-time' person in order to impress
3 Always ask what is required and listen to the answer before you play or sing
4 Sketch out the piece with very simple parts and concentrate on getting a good feel
5 Keep it exciting – choose your moment to rip and don't underplay
6 Don't be a pest. After the audition leave and follow up with a phone call a few days later

Auditioning by post

You have heard through the grapevine or the classifieds that a famous band or solo artist are looking for a new musician to flesh out the touring band. They are looking specifically for a rhythm guitarist and you believe that you are the person for the job. So what do you do? You get out your guitar, put your amp in front of your ghettoblaster, play every Steve Vai-style lick and solo that you can think of, write your name on the tape, pop it into a brown envelope, send it off and wait for the 'when can you start letter'... congratulations, you have just failed the audition!

If someone's after a rhythm guitarist, backing vocalist or a percussionist give them exactly that. At the Academy students are encouraged to record audition-friendly demos. A typical session demo for a bass player might be: four or five styles, demonstrated to a click or quality drum track. Each example might be sixteen bars long – eight bars played simply followed by eight bars with fills. The philosophy is to give the listener something to hang on to, that will give them a reason to listen to at least another 30 seconds of your tape, and you're in with a chance. Also, when you are sending in a tape use a little lateral thinking and consider how you are going to package it. Good, creative packaging will get you noticed and also show you have attention to detail and that you are organised as well. You are dealing with art and artists so think about how you are going to project yourself. Use your imagination to project your character, make it fun.

One example of this is a student from the Academy who went for the job of second guitar with Bernard Butler (ex-Suede, McAlmont and Butler). He styled the whole package on the theme of 'Reservoir Dogs' with a photo of himself tied up, being tortured and having water thrown over his face. The vibe of the package was that he had to get the job to escape the torture! Remember that your self-promotion must not finish once you've recorded your demo tape, make them want to pick out your tape because of its packaging. This rule should apply to all tapes that you send, be they for auditions, record companies or management companies.

Tim Pearson session guitarist – how did he land that Boyzone gig?

Kevin Nixon, of Major Minor management, had this to say about demo presentation:

> 'The best demo package I have received recently was from a band called 'Tangerine'. They had themed the package so that it was like a Christmas stocking with real presents alongside information about the band. Right at the bottom of the stocking was their demo CD and a Tangerine. Of course the whole thing leapt out of the week's pile of tapes and CDs and demanded to be listened to. This was where the band fell down. The track wasn't any good. Their 'limiting factor' was the music but had they got that together their presentation was striking enough to draw attention to the music. Of course it's no use drawing attention to something if it's not amazing.'

So now we have created a monster band. We've chopped and changed, analysed, experimented and now hopefully have created the 'ultimate success machine' – a creative unit capable of going all the way. Now we know where we want to go, but the route may be a little unclear. Where on earth do we start? We will start with a plan.

Mapping and planning

aving analysed and defined our project we can take this firm foundation and begin to build a sensible career path. So many of an artist's responsibilities revolve around creating a set of aims, which can be systematically achieved, with the help of the creative and management teams built around the act. In order to create a series of realistic and attainable goals, which can then be put into chronological order, it would be advisable to work through the following steps:

- Analysis of those around you – do you understand the strengths and weaknesses of your team, and are their roles clearly defined?
- Route mapping – what's the process involved in making it happen?

It's so hard to be objective when you are actually involved with your own project. The danger is, of course, over estimating the quality of your work and wasting time 'treading water' when you need to be moving forwards creatively and professionally at a rate of knots. Peter Henderson (Academy of Contemporary Music graduate and band leader) went through the classic learning curves of a young artist and had this to say on the importance of planning:

'When we started our first band we didn't really have a plan, in fact we didn't even think we needed one. The band was called 'Choke' and we recorded a demo tape which we all thought was great. My Dad helped us out and we pressed up a couple of thousand CDs and prepared to be 'discovered'. Of course what happened was that two months after the first recording the band was twice as good, with better songs, new members and a better look. In the meantime we had sold a hundred or so CDs to friends and family and I've still got the rest of them under the bed. Rather than make the same mistakes again the band decided to sit down with the team at the Academy and make a sensible career plan that would have more chance of being ultimately successful and hopefully less expensive.

We came to realise that the stuff that is dealt with in the beginning of this book, actually deciding what you are, what you do and making sure that it is viable is so incredibly important. We could see all the other local acts falling into these negative cycles of demoing, gigging, doing photos and then going in a completely new direction (usually led by the singer or guitarist) making the promo materials obsolete. Sitting down with Bruce at the Academy we started to really look at what we were doing. He forced us to look at every aspect of the project objectively. 'Choke' for example is a pretty dodgy name but when we were actually using that name we somehow convinced ourselves it was OK. We renamed ourselves and really defined and narrowed down the direction to very poppy indie guitar rock. We analysed what we were happy with creatively and who our market would hopefully be. From this point we were actually in good shape to put together a serious, workable plan.'

Organising and team roles

When going through the mapping and planning stage of your project it's important to recognise that time and energy are everything. So far in this chapter we've been looking at the product and making sure that it all ties up. It is vital that you ensure that both available time and resources are managed effectively. Time and energy invested in planning before you start the practical application of actually 'doing it' will save money and wasted effort by anticipating problems before they occur. For example: Bands 'A' and 'B' have both managed to blag their way onto a local festival bill here's how they deal with it:

Band A

Have planned the gig, taken the promoter out for a beer and understand what's required of them. They know the venue, stage and have planned where everyone's going to be. Upon arriving at the venue each member of the band offloads the backline to a designated and confined area. The drummer sets up the core elements of the kit whilst the bandleader trots off and introduces himself to the soundman to ascertain what beer he drinks. Guitar and bass boys have painstakingly trained their best mates to understand the intricacies of backline set up and general guitar maintenance. The net result, when the stage manager shouts 'band A sound check, you've got five minutes' the backline goes up without a hitch, guitars are in tune, guitarists have picks and spare leads, drummer has sticks, and singer is in the right place at the right time.

Band B

These guys go for a different approach. They can't find the venue because everyone thought that someone else was 'doing it'. When they arrive the singer goes 'for a leak' and isn't seen again during the whole off loading procedure. Gear comes off the van and is chucked all over the venue and the drummer takes the opportunity to comment that the PA sounds 'bol...ks' with the sound man standing just behind him. The net result, when the stage manager shouts 'band B sound check, you've got five minutes' the band can't find their gear, some of it's been loaded into the PA company's trucks, the singer can't be found, the promoter's pulling his hair out and the soundman doesn't give a toss because he has every intention of being in the bar when band B are doing their thing anyway.

TIP

*W*hen doing shows/gigs make life easy for yourself by making it easy for those around you.

One of the main issues that tends to set bands on a course for self-destruct is that it all becomes very personal, roles are undefined and situations that arise are always someone else's fault. Most successful companies have complete structure to their projects before they commence with clearly defined roles for each team member. Whoever is designated the leader/manager of the band should be able to answer the question, 'Who's responsible for getting a satisfactory result on each specified job for the task in hand?'

Professional bands should think of themselves as small businesses and as part of this process each person has a role to fulfil not only as a musician but also as a member of the team. In a business situation it's important to ascertain all the various tasks that need to be completed in order to achieve the overall objective, then assess who's available to do the work, what their natural abilities are and then fit the correct person to each job. Typical tasks that need to be sorted out include:

Project management

Most bands have a natural leader, this often falls to the person, or persons, with the creative vision for the music. This person should also be able to motivate a team, assign roles and help the individuals achieve satisfactory results.

Bookings (studio and gigs)

The person responsible for bookings will need to have drive and determination, negotiating and organisational skills. It will be enormously helpful to have the use of a computer to compile a database of venues, agents and record gig fees etc.

Press and advertising

One band member should be responsible for generating publicity. This individual will need a creative ability, good use of language and the imagination to cook up a story out of, or put a spin on, daily events. The ability to take usable press photographs is a distinct advantage.

Equipment and travel

Whether it's cars, a transit van, tour bus or Concorde, someone still needs to make the arrangements and ensure that nothing is left behind. Usually one band member is responsible for route planning and making sure that everyone gets out of bed and arrives on time. If you plan on running a band vehicle this will have to be maintained, taxed and MOT'd. The person in charge of transport will have to liaise with the financial controller in the band to make sure that the money is made available for these inevitable costs.

Merchandise

Design, production and selling are important issues and someone needs to be in charge. This role can be farmed out to a person outside the band if needs be, but will have to be co-ordinated by a team member.

Financial control

This is just a glorified role for the band accountant, who keeps a record of all funds into and out of the band account. It would be sensible practice for the band to meet once a month and discuss the state of the band's finances and plan the next month's spending in advance. This role will require a person who is disciplined, honest and has the capability to attend to minute detail.

TIP

Whatever the booking arrangements are, make sure that you have a standard outline letter of agreement confirming them. This saves all sorts of arguments later on.

TIP

Generate a simple form outlining all the gear needed for your show – the equipment manager can check it off at the following times:

- Loading
- Get in
- Get out
- Off loading

This way you are less likely to forget or lose expensive kit.

Defining roles and assigning jobs avoids the frustrating scenario of one or two individuals doing far more work than the other members of the act. In the real world you probably will find that there will always be an unequal division of labour but this type of planning should help keep that to a minimum.

Time and project management

Now that you have created a great project and have allocated roles to the team members you need to put some thought into ways to maximise the use of your time and resources.

A band that seriously aspires to international success has a long and difficult journey ahead of them and must work at many times the rate of their competitors. In order to work at our full potential we need to take some tips from the pros on how to manage the most precious of all our resources: time.

Critical path analysis

It is crucial that you understand the overall aims and objectives before starting out. This considered, the team leader needs to have an effective control mechanism to ensure a systematic approach to achieving the goals. For example when starting a band project in which order should the tasks be completed? How long should each job take? And in what time frame should the tasks be completed etc. Once these questions have been asked the project leader can then establish a realistic pattern of work and delegate the tasks according to the designated role of each team member. Many new bands don't plan the timing of individual elements of the project before commencing. Once it's on its way they find that jobs are completed in the wrong order, or half way through a task the band leader/manager discovers that it cannot be completed because another job needs to be done first.

To help in this organisation you could consider using a Critical Path Analysis chart (CPA) to establish the best method for multi-tasking. This simple control document lists all tasks to be completed on the left-hand side of the page (vertical) and all days/weeks or months available across the top of the page (horizontal). The band leader then shades the appropriate boxes giving a clear visual indication of how long each job will take and the specific order in which each should be undertaken. In addition to this the manager can also see at a glance any time windows that are empty and is then able to timetable tasks into these slots.

A CPA on the wall detailing a band's career aims over a 12 month period is a great motivator as well as an efficient way to monitor your act's working practice. If you fall behind on your targets of goals that you need to achieve by certain times you will be instantly aware of the situation and can adjust your working practice accordingly.

Job description

Week	1	2	3	4	5	6	7	8	9	10	11	12	13	14	15	16	17	18	19	...	52
Book rehearsal studio	•																				
Devise set list				•																	
Rehearse material		•	•	•	•	•	•	•													
Write originals		•	•	•	•	•	•	•													
Define direction	•																				
Design merchandise			•	•																	
Book gigs	•	•	•																		
Plan press campaign		•	•																		
Organise press											•										
Photo session										•											
Book demo studio									•												
Play gigs (tour)												•	•	•	•	•	•	•	•		•
Record demo											•										
Package demo												•									
Collect merchandise												•									

The above example is not meant to be definitive by any means but is designed give you an idea of how the overall shape of the project can be viewed at a glance. In addition to this the team instantly becomes accountable to a time frame and can measure its actual progress against planned performance. The CPA illustrated also gives the band a clear picture of when the busiest times are and any available windows for extra tasks etc. From here the bandleader can easily split the tasks into the related roles and designate to each member of the team a set time frame within which to work. Loads of time and many disagreements can be avoided. Individual tasks can all be broken down into steps and put into their own CPAs by the individuals responsible for their completion. You should now have a clear understanding of the following: product and the marketplace, effective use of band members and time, team roles and project management.

Of course this doesn't sound very rock 'n' roll, and smart bands are keen to maintain the illusion. Your fans don't want to find out that running a band is just like running any other business because it's mundane and boring. Naive young bands fall for the hype and spend their time being disorganised thinking that that's what rock 'n' roll is about. Actually rock 'n' roll is about *appearing* to be disorganised – but that's our little secret.

Wes is the general manager of Mushroom records and responsible for the marketing strategy behind numerous multi-platinum acts including: Ash, Garbage and Peter Andre. Wes had this to say on the thinking behind some of his successful campaigns.

'Firstly there must be a strategy on signing new artists. Mushroom have a variety of different artists on its roster at any one time so we may be more reluctant than a specialist label to signing say an indie band if we're already working one. We have a definite strategic plan and when we sign an artist they become part of that plan so it's important to us that everybody from myself to the accounts team are behind and for the act.

The next step is to link the newly signed artist to a specific market and media, for example, with Garbage it's 7 inch singles, lots of formats, indie vibe, advertising and promotions in Melody Maker, Kerrang – publications like that. However if you take Christian Fry then we're looking at a different approach completely, different formats, with publicity targeted at Smash Hits and TOTP's magazine. So yeah, identifying the correct market for an act and making sure that their music, image and live show tie in are all really important.

The process for breaking a new artist is once again very structured. Take Christian again, we had him on a big tour last April, Summer Road Shows, School tours and then he did the Boyzone tour in September/October timed with the release of the first single. Actually during this time he was working five appearances a day, two schools, regional radio, Boyzone and then off to an under 18's club for another show. All this was carefully planned along with detailed promotions through radio, TV and press. Bands who want to get a record deal should be planning to get in front of the scouts by playing the hip clubs in London like the Waterrats or the Barfly, bring their local following down to create a buzz, get noticed. Most importantly get a good manager as quickly as possible because most companies in this industry deal with people that they know and trust.'

If all this preparation and planning sounds a bit like hard work – that's because it is. Remember this when the going gets tough – if you aren't prepared to do it there are plenty of bands out there who are. In music it's not so much he who dares wins, as he who can be arsed wins.

3 ★

Management

Many young bands are not quite clear on what a manager is or exactly what these mysterious people do. The authors of this book are used to being passed a dodgy first demo tape from a band who haven't yet done their first gig and hearing that this fledgling act are hot on the trail of getting a 'manager'. It's almost as if that by taking on that title a normal human being can assume supernatural powers to:

- get gigs
- make the band better looking
- turn the demo into a collection of hit singles
- get record deals
- generally take responsibility for providing a career for the band

These bands miss the point. Having or not having a good manager does not diminish your responsibilities as an artist (which you will be fully aware of having read the first three chapters). A manager's primary role is to 'look after the welfare of the artist'. This is an extremely broad set of responsibilities which will vary with individual artists and may include: personal counselling, business planning, help with song writing problems and protecting the artist from pressure from record companies and of course actually negotiating record, publishing and merchandising deals. Most managers will earn more than the individual band members they manage will, but, if they're any good, they will be working a lot harder and they will be worth it.

As an artist you will have goals which are both creative and professional. It is your manager's job to take those goals, put them into chronological order and make sure that the practicalities are realistic and obtainable. These goals may range from a gig at Camden's Rock Garden to an international hit single, and in an ideal world you will be working systematically together to achieve these aspirations. The point is, it is difficult to help a musician who doesn't really know what they want or where they are going.

The manager will also be in a position to 'plug the gaps' in an act. He or she will have the benefit of being able to observe the band from outside the unit and so is in a position to objectively comment on the quality of their work. A good manager will also probably have more life experience than the band ,who may well be very young and in need of guidance from a reliable stable source. All obstacles can be overcome with the right team. For example:

> **TIP**
>
> If the goals are unclear then it is impossible for the manager to plan a strategy to achieve them.

The Armadillos

Band A 'The Armadillos' are hip, hot and happening. Only problem is they just can't write a hit single. They can overcome this if the manager can be objective enough to find the problem and suggest a possible solution. In The Armadillos' case the singer 'Ant Eater' (who looks great, and is very popular with all the female fans) writes all the lyrics.

Our wise old manager has identified that the problem is that poor old Ant has lived at home with his parents for eighteen years and hasn't got much to write about. His melodies, however, are fantastic. The manager saves the day and comes up with a plan to get Ant to write with another lyricist to combine what he does have going for him (great melodies and a great band) with what he doesn't – strong subject matter.

The Spleens

Band B 'The Spleens' are an out and out punk band. The songs are amazing, the direction perfect for the time, they look great and sell records by the bucket load. Only problem is the singer and guitarist argue like cat and dog. The constant disputes threaten the stability of the band. The manager must ' plug the gap' and firstly identify the problem, in this case lack of stability, and then suggest a solution.

In The Spleens' case the manager examines the situation and concludes that the two musicians need a stiff talking to and are simply behaving in a childish way.

This man is not a Spleen

What qualities do we need in a manager?

Most artists in the know would put 'experience' high on the list of priorities required for successful management. To be effective in the role a manager has to have a much broader range of expertise than nearly anyone else in the business does. Imagine going from a meeting with the marketing department on single formats in the record company to tidying up the finer points of a publishing deal with a lawyer. Then imagine attending a meeting on press interviews with the press department, followed by another meeting on choosing a producer for the album with the A&R department all in the space of one day.

A manager must be able to speak with authority and wisdom in all these situations and must have the experience to back up his decision making. It is almost impossible to learn 'on the job' there simply isn't enough time or leeway to make mistakes. Many people who are successful in this role have had a wide range of relevant music business experience. Kevin Nixon (Major Minor Management) for example has:

- been an artist signed to a major label
- spent thousands of hours in the studio
- produced hit records
- run two independent record labels
- been an A&R consultant
- had a string of successful artists on his management roster

This level of expertise in the management of an act will give a record company confidence that there is a steady hand at the wheel.

You may be asking a label to invest at least half a million pounds on breaking a new act. Before that level of investment takes place most MD's in major labels will be looking for a solid management situation. It is at this stage, when an act's career becomes a serious business, that the 'deadwood' in the project has to be removed. Weak band members will get replaced and inexperienced managers will get the sack.

Age can become an issue at this point. Most experienced artists would be wary of employing a manager who is very young as the likelihood of them having gathered not only professional experience, but also the life skills needed to cope with the demands of the job, will be remote. A manager will often have to make crucial decisions under difficult circumstances and cope with extraordinary pressure. At these times in an act's career the last thing we need is the captain of the ship having a nervous breakdown!

As well as the professional qualifications, managers need to have certain personal skills:

> **TIP**
>
> The reality of the situation is harsh but from your point of view, as the artist, your own professional survival will depend to a large degree on the competence of your manager.

Honesty

The reputation of managers as a professional body took a hit in the sixties when it was commonplace to hear of artists being ripped off and dodgy deals being done. This old fashioned view still survives outside the industry, but is actually misinformed in reality. The music business is a relatively small industry, and a manager with a reputation for dishonesty would not be able to practise with any degree of longevity. Kevin Nixon explains his philosophy:

'You can only survive if you are honest and your reputation is that you are honest, that is probably the most important thing. Also, you've got to be able to evolve, because I've just signed a new act recently and two of the members of the band are 18 year old girls, but I'm 42! So you can't be unaware of what it is that 18 year old people want to talk about and are into, what motivates them. You can't just retire to the golf course at 40 and think it's all going to be great, if you're going to be in management you've got to understand what's going on all the time. So consequently those 18 year old girls have to feel properly represented by me, not just on the music but about everything they're doing. I'm quite lucky because I've got children of that age and that helps me stay plugged in.

The music business is a very young industry, it only started in the fifties as we know it. So it's 40 years old and for the first time you're getting dinosaur managers as well as dinosaur artists, there's never been such a thing, and the dinosaur managers that I know have great difficulty identifying with young bands. If your going to work with new and young artists you've got to go out there and find out what it is they're doing and what they're into. That's the key to continuing to have success.'

Tenacity

It's a tough old world out there and a manager is going to have to
deal with some heavy weight situations which will need a degree of
resilience, even aggression, to cope with. If you were wrongly
accused of a serious crime and were facing a prison sentence you
would want your defence lawyer to have certain skills to be able to
handle the situation. These same skills: intellect, articulation,
toughness and even the ability to intimidate others are going to be
vital when asserting the interests of the band in a confrontation
with key players in the record company.

Kevin Nixon

Don't forget that the important figures in the music business have
survived and prospered in one of the most competitive arenas in the
world. These people are unlikely to be pushovers. One of the
authors recalls observing Kevin Nixon having to deal with a variety
of confrontational situations:

> 'The band was playing Manchester Apollo and we rolled up to the
> soundcheck a bit later than usual. On the way in we noticed a trio
> of big guys selling bootleg mugs with the band's logo stamped on
> them. While we were soundchecking Kev nipped out and, not only
> did he send them packing, but he confiscated the entire vanload of
> mugs single-handedly. The only problem then was what to do with
> all those bloody mugs!
>
> On another occasion we had a fan in the dressing room who
> wouldn't leave. After a few gentle hints that we needed to get ready
> to go on stage we actually asked him firmly to leave. He became
> aggressive and Kev stepped in very quickly, felled him with one
> blow and had him out the door and down the stairs before he had
> time to react. It wasn't pretty but managers have got to be able to
> handle that kind of stuff.'

The best managers have been involved in the business of music for many years and have therefore had the opportunity to make every mistake that can be made, and consequently will be able to advise you on what not to do as well as what to do. A manager will place a 'structure' round a band, including the right team of people, the right record company, the right agent, the right accountant, etc.

A manager will also protect his fledgling outfit, acting as a first line of defence, not only from outside forces, but also from themselves. The key word is guidance, and in a perfect world a band would have a manager right from the beginning protecting them and helping them to achieve their potential. But many bands believe that a good lawyer is more important than a good manager and this has changed the working face of the music industry, constructing limitations within an industry that, it must be remembered, is still essentially built around the artistry of musicians.

Major Minor Management

Many lawyers are insensitive to the subtleties of the creative processes, and for many it is seen as a way of getting paid quickly. This appears to have been motivated partly by the American penchant for legal disputes that can lead to big payouts, but it is also a result of paranoia motivated by a mixture of past horror stories and modern day mistrust between parties believing that they are being ripped off. It is important that there is an element of trust between involved parties and a good rapport between artist and manager is essential. Kevin Nixon advises:

'try and pick people that you would want to go to the pub with, if you do not trust the person that you are working with you should not be working with them.'

Some managers insist on forging a relationship with their acts initially, without producing a binding contract. A good and trustworthy manager should be happy to have this form of initial 'trial period' to work with the act and see how it goes. Having said this there are few managers who will continue to act for a growing band without eventually negotiating a contract that is mutually agreeable.

Working to a game plan

Along with experience, managers should also have vision. They will listen to what their artist wants, help to redirect any misguided preconceptions and generally give the act an idea of what he or she believes they should be doing. The manager will then take this information away, expand on it and turn it into a plan that can then be interpreted by record companies, publishing companies and agencies that actually means something other than 'lets make an album and go on tour'... which is not a plan. They must find a way of getting through the Snakes and Ladders game that is the music industry and ensure that the public becomes aware of their act in the most efficient way. Record companies in particular love a manager who arrives on their doorstep with a clear strategy that they can understand and that they think will work. However if a manager arrives expecting the record label to come up with all the ideas, it is highly likely that the deal will fall through.

Music business 1-0 management

When it comes to positioning management within the realms of the music industry as a whole, it is not always given the respect that is rightly deserves. Kevin Nixon described the position of real managers, as he sees it, thus:

> 'I would say that management is the Barnsley of the record business! It is the absolute unsung hero, the least celebrated and definitely the least appreciated. I'll give you an example, it's a bit of a negative example but it's a good one. If an artist wants to fire his manager he just walks into his lawyer and it's a done deal, if an artist wants to get rid of his record company ... impossible! No lawyer will ever take it on unless there is some glaringly obvious thing where he can just deal with it. Same with a publishing company, and it's incredibly wrong because good managers are the true A&R people of the music business. They are the ones that go out and find the acts that the labels miss.
>
> When I walk into a label with a band, the first question I always ask is 'how come you don't know about them?' They have several A&R levels there so there's no reason at all why they shouldn't know about everything that's going on. It's always quite an attractive thing when I've got an artist that they don't know about because I feel I've got the upper hand from day one. Record companies expect us to be there and expect us to make all these plans and do all the things that we do, but they often don't want to pay for it. It's a real thorn in my side. The industry needs to support us more because there's an awful lot of people out there doing it who are hopeless and unqualified.'

Why you?

So the question that must be asked is why would a manager be interested in taking on and representing a particular band or act? There is no magic answer and no big mystery to be unravelled. A manager is just like any of the other individuals in the business who you will have to convince to invest time or money or both into your project. They are all looking for quality music that they believe in and that they can also sell. If a band has no 'limiting factors' and are well defined, good writers, commercially viable, look good and

Jack Cooke from Radiator – definitely defined

can play then there is no reason why professionals in the business will not want to become involved.

In many instances we will discover that success will hinge not on giving industry key players a reason to become involved with the project (all bands have something good about them), but rather making sure that there are no reasons for these people not to get involved. Until the band has developed to a reasonable level of viability most artists will be faced with the choice of either sitting around doing very little or managing themselves.

Self-management

A band can effectively manage themselves in the early part of their careers. This is good practice and not only gives the band a greater understanding of how the business works, but it also brings home the enormous amount of work required to achieve even the most modest of goals.

Economics

So how much does it cost to employ a manager? Most managers commission a standard 20 per cent of an artist's earnings. This means that 20 per cent of everything you earn, including: royalties, advances, sponsorship, merchandising and gig fees will be commissioned. A good manager is worth his weight in gold, and 80 per cent of a lot is infinitely preferable to 100 per cent of not much.

A gross miscalculation

Beware! The figure 20 per cent can mean different things to different managers. The two key words from our point of view are 'gross' and 'net'. A management contract where the commission is calculated on the gross is going to be considerably more expensive than another contract where the commission is calculated on the net. Let me give you an example.

Band A 'The Three Legged Dogs' have toured the UK for three weeks and generated 100k in gig fees. They have a gross management deal and their manager Mr. Sharky immediately commissions 20 per cent of the fees and pockets 20 grand. Unfortunately the tour expenses have come in at 95k and this leaves the band with only 5k profit and, after paying Mr. Sharky, they are left with a 15k loss.

Band B 'The Four Legged Dogs' are in a much better position. As well as having an extra leg they have a management contract based on 20 per cent of the net profit. On the same gig fees The Four Legged Dogs' manager (Mr. Reasonable) commissions only on the net profit (which is 5k) and so presents a much more palatable bill of 1k to the band. So instead of a loss, the four band members come out with a small profit of 1k each.

What a difference those two little words 'gross' and 'net' make. Imagine the nightmare scenario of a hugely successful act that make bigger and bigger losses as the size of the gigs they play increases. When you sign your first management contract you will need legal advice. A contract will be complex, hard to read and easy to misinterpret and so professional legal help will be needed to help you understand exactly what you are signing (more details in Legal Eagles, Chapter 10). But if you ask your lawyer about nothing else, enquire which parts of your income will be commissioned on the gross profit and which part on the net. It could make all the difference.

Creating a buzz

Buzz is a key word in the music industry and, to put it bluntly, bands with a 'buzz' get signed and the others do not. So how do you go about creating a 'buzz' for your act? The first thing to understand is that if there are any fundamental problems with the band, i.e. a lack of definition, then no amount of hype will be effective. It is unlikely that any amount of great marketing will be able to turn what is essentially a pub band into the next big thing because it is very difficult to fake it, the band must have some substance to it. A 'buzz' is a feeling of excitement within the industry, the music press and the public. All those groups of people are very discerning and are only going to get genuinely excited about an act if they are very special indeed. So if it can be assumed that your band has substance and is the business (and you must be objective with yourself about this) then what follows is a standard pathway to getting noticed.

There are other routes to a record deal but this structured approach works very well for live based acts, putting the control of your act's destiny in your own hands. We create a series of goals, leading to a recording contract or a hit record, which can then be put into a chronological order.

Working backwards from our primary aims it is then a logical progression, with the band systematically attaining each goal. This will give your band the motivation to be constantly moving forward, thus removing the possibility of the act 'waiting around' for someone to come out of the blue and offer a management deal or a record deal which may never happen.

Make it big in a little town

Down the pub – it may seem small time – but by playing a humble pub gig you are following in the footsteps of countless legendary artists

The first step for your newly formed band is simply to create a local following. This may sound like an easy thing to do, but if you take a town like Guildford as an example (this is where the Academy of Contemporary Music is based) there are around 300 or 400 fairly serious local bands in the city and its surrounding area. The chances are that there are at least another 500 bands that are still in their formative stages. So there are hundreds of bands out there all trying to play live gigs – but there are very few venues for these bands to play.

We live in an age where there is so much great music easily available (you just have to put on the radio to hear good music for free), and it is now very difficult to convince people to actually go and see a band live, particularly if they will have to pay for it.

It is also a sad fact that most people have had bad experiences with live music, seeing local bands play and having to endure drab sets, extreme volume and terrible sound. All of this leads to an awful night out for the punter whose perception of what a local gig could be is then tainted by bad experience. There are many obstacles that need to be overcome just to get people through the door to see your gig.

Causing a stir

We are initially faced with two problems: making sure that our band is good enough to create a stir or a 'buzz' on a local level, and ensuring that we have the mechanisms in place to publicise our activities, raise profile and generate awareness of our activities. Local punters are just as discerning and hard to please as any other section of society, and many other bands will be competing for the reputation of 'hottest local act'. Your first gigs will probably be performances to family and friends. It will quickly become apparent that you will need to expand on this limited support if you are to progress. When we can guarantee a crowd of at least 200 people then we will have achieved our first objective. If we have done our homework and analysed our 'limiting factors' and streamlined our approach, as discussed in Chapter 1, we will be ahead of the other local bands. Hopefully the quality of our work will stand out from the local mire of average bands with ideas above their abilities.

One of the biggest mistakes that most bands make is that they just go and do a gig without considering how they are going to present the performance. This is where lateral thinking and a psychological approach to handling an audience can pay off. If you can find a way to make people who didn't attend your gig feel like they have missed out on something special, they are likely to make the effort to attend the next one. You need to create a little bit of

Moby – there's always one
who lowers the tone ...
*Pics courtesy Adam
Friedberg*

demand or a mini-buzz in the local area. How are you going to do
this? It is a good idea to ensure that something unusual happens at
your gig. Remember that in rock 'n roll sex, nudity and outrage
often work wonders. The first punk who threw up on stage started a
performance revolution and received a vast amount of press. The
first man to wear a dress (possibly Ozzy Osbourne originally, and
later Kurt Cobain) also received spectacular press coverage.
Obviously to recreate these particular examples would be pointless
now due to their over-exposure, but the first people to pull these
stunts achieved two results; they shocked and entertained
audiences, and got vast amounts of press.

Think carefully about every detail of your presentation. Is it
really necessary to have a support band for example? Most support
bands are too loud, play too long, aren't very good and don't pull
many punters. How about thinking of a different angle to this,
substituting the obligatory support band with something else like a
performance artist or a poet perhaps.

One of the authors played in a band called 'b.l.o.w'. This band
had a roadie who used to hand out proverbs to everybody who came
through the door, another of the authors was in a band called 'This
Witness' which had a Spanish guitarist playing while people came
into the venue and then opened their set accompanied by a fire
breather. This may sound like hype but the end result was that
people would leave the gigs and then go and talk about it with their
friends.

TIP

*U*se lateral thinking
to create not just a
gig but an event, a
'vibe' that will make
people regret that they
missed the gig and
anxious not to miss
out on the next one.

Making the news

It is vital to learn how the local press works and use it to your advantage. If anything at all happened at your gig that could be considered even slightly controversial then make sure that it goes in the local paper. Local papers are very easy to get press stories into, but do not bother with an official style 'press release' as these are usually incredibly boring and un-newsworthy. Every band sends in a press release which says some thing like 'we are playing down the Cricketers and it will be great'. While this will get you into the local gig list it is not exactly awe inspiring or effective advertising.

Bruce Dickinson recalls a local press campaign that was spectacularly effective for his old band 'Little Angels'.

'We were still at school and had played our local theatre bar several times. It sold out every time, which wasn't really a big deal as the capacity was only about 100 or so. In a fit of wild optimism we booked a large hall called The Opera House with a capacity of 1300. It was only later when we had committed ourselves that we realised what an ambitious task it would be to fill the place. We had two choices – either play to an embarrassingly small crowd or do some serious publicity. We decided to go for it and blitz the town over the following month with promotion and advertising to try and fill the gig. This was the plan:

1 Tour the local schools playing charity gigs at lunchtimes
2 Fly post the town with 200 posters
3 Invent a press story and create an ongoing controversy in the letters page
4 Ask local businesses to sponsor the gig with a full page advert in the local paper
5 Hand out leaflets in the town centre dressed in gorilla costumes (I kid you not)

'The council did us a big favour when they threatened to take us to court over the fly posters. We exaggerated the situation and invented a press story saying that we would be fined £400 for every poster. The local paper was happy to do a photograph session of us taking the posters down. We quickly followed this up with a stream of letters from our supporters to the paper saying what a disgrace it was that a young band who were showing such get up and go should be threatened with legal action etc. Disappointingly most people seemed to agree and to keep the controversy raging we were forced to write letters under assumed names saying what hooligans we were for putting the posters up in the first place. The end result was that any one living in our hometown couldn't escape hearing about the gig. We ended up with a crowd of 1000 people – not bad for a local band in a seaside town with a population of 50,000 (most of whom are retired). That turned out to be an incredibly important period in the band's career. That one gig was the springboard for an independent record deal and forged the foundations of a relationship with our manager. I don't think we would have had a career in music if we had made the decision to cancel that gig and not go for it.

My advice to young bands regarding press would be this: It's actually incredibly easy to get local press for the simple reason that not much generally happens. The Scarborough Evening News for example comes out every day. Imagine trying to get enough interesting copy to fill that local paper every day – it must be very difficult. If a band can provide good quality stories with an angle for a photograph it's bound to go in. How could it not? To make doubly sure word process your story and present it already written on disc and provide quality shots yourself. A hard pressed over-worked journalist with a deadline to meet will welcome anything that makes life easier.'

Check the set

Once you have a reputation for creating interesting stories and possibly a bit of controversy this will generate more awareness and hopefully more people wanting to come to your gigs. Having got the punters through the door, the band needs to be good enough to blow the audience away ensuring that the buzz on the band continues to build. Professional acts are aware of how crucial the order of the set is to the flow of the gig; most amateur bands rarely give this any serious thought at all. In fact the order of the songs is far more important to the feel of the performance than how well the band plays. If you get it right and build a set properly it will make a massive difference to the enjoyment factor of the audience.

You must use your self-management skills, be objective and study how you could improve the band and its performance potential as a whole. Get a friend to video the set in rehearsal and experiment not only with the order of the set but also the way songs are linked together. Details like count-ins, what the singer says to introduce the song and tempos are well worth rehearsing until the performances are solid.

Strangely, the better rehearsed and prepared an act is the more spontaneous they can afford to be onstage, confident in the knowledge that they can always fall back onto familiar ground if they need to. A confident count in from a solid drummer, at the right tempo will start the song off on a firm foundation. A nervous drummer clicking sticks with no verbal 'one, two, three, four' count may make the band come into the song hesitantly, unsure which beat is beat one. Many drummers even speed up within their count, bringing the song in at an artificially fast tempo.

TIP

Many drummers use an electronic metronome to reference the correct tempo.

When playing live the adrenaline produced will speed up your reactions making fast tempos seem slower. Record your gigs and you may be surprised at how the band races through the set sounding scrappy and out of control. If you watch acts that are used to playing stadiums you may notice how steady they tend to be with their tempos. Rushed, out of control performances come over particularly badly on big stages. The key word is control – if a band is in command of its tempos then this will communicate to the audience who will then relax into the performance.

Nothing spreads quicker than panic – many of us can recall an uncomfortable feeling watching an inexperienced performer, perhaps a comedian, flounder. Compare this with the feeling of observing a professional comedian at ease, timing relaxed and fully in control of the gig. Two different performers, possibly performing the same material in two different ways. The effect on the audience is completely different.

We are now at the point where all our hard work will be paying dividends. The band is lean, honed and focused. The direction is as sharp and clear. The set contains some amazing career breaking tracks and we have eliminated all our limiting factors. Not only are we easily the best band in the area but the local population know all about our activities and we have achieved a certain level of notoriety. If we are not pulling crowds of at least two hundred or so people by this stage it may be wise to re read chapter one and re-asses the viability of the project. If we cannot create interest on a local level can we realistically expect to do the same nationally?

Capitalising on your success

If you are really serious about creating a buzz in the music business with management companies and record labels, then it is time to take the principles that have already been a practical success, and apply them in the capital city. One of the best assets you possess when making the move into London is the local following that you already have, because once you have landed gigs at various credible venues, you will be able to bring 50 people or so on a coach.

The sort of places you should be playing are venues like The Splash Club, The Orange, The Garage, Subterrainia, The King's Head, The Powerhaus, etc. However the best way to find out the happening venues of the moment is to look in the back of Kerrang, Melody Maker or NME. See which venues crop up time and time again and then get a gig there. All the practice that you have in creating opportunities for the band will come in useful at this stage because it can be quite tricky to get a foot in the door at these venues. Nobody said that it would be easy and all these obstacles that you will overcome may prove too much for most of your competitors. In some ways the harder the path the easier it is for the bands who do have what it takes to shine through.

To begin with you will probably be given a Monday night at 7.30pm, but if you want another gig at that venue on a Friday or Saturday at 9.00pm you must get people through the door of that venue on that dull, rainy Monday night. If you do not bother getting your local fans to come to this first gig because it is hard work organising a coach and mailing out to your database then you will not get another gig there. Of course what you are really aiming to do in the long term is to generate a buzz in the Capital.

If you are now a great band and you have developed your craft on a local level then this can and will happen if you continue to improve and tighten up your act. Bands who are creating a buzz can feel the excitement building around the act, bands who aren't just play a few gigs to less and less people feeling like they are wading through treacle. A genuine 'buzz' takes on a life of its own and is self perpetuating, feeding and growing on the excitement generated by the act.

Once you are playing in London you will be relying on your local following for your first few gigs. After a while you will hopefully not need to rely on this and be able to play gigs under your own steam, and real paying punters will come out to see you. But imagine how special you have got to be to pull this off. There are so many gigs going on in London, hundreds every night, that it is going to be very hard work to stand out from the crowd. But if you have the discipline to constantly raise standards and levels of presentation and music and keep on top of current trends you are going to be in with a very real chance of success. Luckily most of your competitors, even in the capital, won't be working that hard. If you cannot picture this happening to your band, then this is how Bruce Dickinson described it,

> 'It happened to the Little Angels, we weren't a particularly great band but we were the right thing at the right time. We used to sell out the Marquee; we used to play there once a week practically. Through the summer of 1987 we got a residency at the Marquee and really built on that, supporting every rock band that came through. After a while we eventually got a headline and sold the club out in the days when the Marquee was a reasonably fashionable venue. If you can do that you're well on the way to getting a record deal. You see the same thing happening today just look at all the bands that have come through the Splash club and got signed.'

Of course there are other ways to creating a 'buzz' and ultimately getting a record deal, but in this book we are going to concentrate on the paths that you, the artist, can control and affect.

Morcheba – a band with a buzz!

Let them come to you

Notice how up until this point you haven't aggressively pursued a record deal, management or publishing contract. In fact you haven't even approached a record company to come and watch a gig. It is a waste of time ringing up an A&R person and saying 'we're playing at the Garage, will you come down and see us?' (this is presuming that you can even make it through to their office, which is unlikely). Far better to concentrate your efforts on building the 'buzz' on the street, for if you have played maybe half a dozen of the right gigs in London then the chances are an A&R person has already seen you.

All the major labels employ A&R people whose aim in life is to find new artists. Many of these professional talent scouts are taking in six gigs a night combing the city seven nights a week. Rest assured eventually you will get seen. The question is not 'will you be discovered' but when you are discovered will you be good enough? If after six months of playing quality venues in the city you have not been approached, it may be wise to spend a little time re-assessing.

Remember that there is a huge gulf between 'record company interest' and a label loading hundreds of thousands of pounds into breaking an act. A junior A&R man will have to convince the head of the A&R department of your viability before the discussions can progress to the next stage. A label with serious intentions may offer to put you in the studio to record some demos, perhaps even with a producer who has a track record. This is an incredibly positive step forward for the band. You will be in a professional studio (probably costing upwards of a £1000 a day) and may even be working with a producer who has been involved with previous hit records.

At this stage it is perfectly within the bounds of possibility that you could get to work with some hot producer. If you know what and who you are looking for the odds of the session being ultimately successful will be increased. This is a very important

TIP

If you are smart you will have been researching the producers responsible for the sounds of the day session for your band's future, and our official advice at this stage is ' don't cock it up!' One of the authors went through this experience three times before eventually signing a record deal.

'We demoed for MCA, someone else who I can't remember and then finally Polydor. The A&R lady, Susan Collins, put us with a producer called Jimbo Barton. This was a smart move and he really whipped a young inexperienced band into shape. He sorted out the arrangement a bit but his main contribution was in tightening the whole thing up and making it sound great sonically. We learned a lot from working with someone who had worked on some big records in the past and what's more we got a record deal out of it!'

National press

While you are actually playing in London you also need to be playing the press game in just the same way that you did in your local area, but this time with the national press. Many people believe that it is incredibly difficult to get into the NME, Kerrang or the Melody Maker, but it is not necessarily the case. The same theory can work for these journalists as it did for the local hacks; they have the same deadlines and the same amount of quality copy to find in a short space of time. So you need to provide them with strong copy because, just as before, standard press releases are no use to either party because millions of bands are submitting identical press releases about their latest single and how great it is. What these journalists need is a spin, a bit of scandal, and some sort of angle. Compare the amount of attention Jarvis Cocker received when Pulp released the classic track 'Common People' and got to number one, with the amount of press he generated by getting onstage with Michael Jackson. Of course somebody is number one in the charts every week but its not every day that somebody shows their arse to Michael Jackson (at least not on national TV!).

Imagination is the key to getting yourself or your band into the national music press. Ideas can come from many sources, but always think laterally and never start a dead end story with a built in sell by date. This means trying to come up with something that can run, a story that can be expanded upon, a story that could take on a life of its own (like the local poster story). A dead end story will only be featured once, but what you really want is one that will give you weeks of coverage. An ideal story is so strong that the national music press will run with it even though the band featured may be relatively unknown.

A great example of how a strong spin on a familiar theme can generate several press pieces is the idea concocted by Bruce's (old

Melody Maker – still incredibly influential after all these years

TIP

Think about two things; what is going to motivate a journalist into wanting to write something about you, and what would you want to read about a band?

and obscure) band b.l.o.w. publicising a support tour. The band were faced with a dilemma in that they were touring on a tight budget and could not afford the money to stay in hotels. Necessity being the mother of invention they released a press story saying that the band would like the tour to have a 'festival vibe' to it and that the band would like fans to send in photographs of their back gardens. The winners of the 'Camping Competition' would have the dubious privilege of letting b.l.o.w. camp in their garden.

The magazines loved the novelty of the idea and ran the story on two pages with photographs. Hundreds of people sent in pictures of their gardens and the band picked ones that were near the venues they were performing at, ensuring also that the people who owned the gardens looked like good fun. They arranged a photo shoot at the beginning of the competition, and then they did a photo shoot during the tour with a review of the gig and an article about the band. Then they followed that up with another article from one particular person's garden. Then three-quarters of the way through the tour somebody had organised for the band to camp in a graveyard in Manchester, which became another press story with pictures.

Out of one piece of lateral thinking the band managed to come up with four or five press stories, this in turn increased the profile of the band which meant that the next press story was easier to get into print. Bruce commented,

'You've just got to come up with these spins on ordinary ideas. Any band can get into any tabloid paper if they come up with something interesting. When I was in the Little Angels I used to ring up a lady called Julia Cutner at the Star and make press stories up. When you start getting in the tabloids, that's when you're really cracking on! You're reaching millions of readers, not just tens of thousands. The daily papers are generally looking for stories on bands that are in the top forty, but anyone can get in if they have a strong enough angle. I used to ring up Julia when ever the Little Angels had a top forty hit and tell her I had some press stories for her. Most of them started with a grain of truth, I'd exaggerate it a bit and then she'd take it and completely blow it up out of all proportion, then you get a great story.

For example, my little brother likes playing on fruit machines, so I told her that he was addicted to amusement arcades. By the time it came out in the Daily Star he'd gambled millions of pounds into fruit machines and was attending Gamblers Anonymous. There was a big photograph of my brother and the caption underneath read 'tragic Jim'! Of course my Granny believes everything she reads in the paper, which caused a few problems and I had to do some explaining. But the main thing was we were in the paper, it got the name about, it might not be the right thing for every band, but to us it was quite funny and I think effective advertising in an indirect way.

I used to give Julia at least six stories and I'd never know which one she'd pick and use. Some were just plain made up, like the one about Mark the drummer. Julia asked me where we had got our new drummer from, and I said that he had been a porn star in Hamburg and he was looking for a change of career. And that was it! It was a flippant comment that got blown up into a story in the Daily Star about his porn days and about how he was doing this rock 'n' roll stuff. Then the story got syndicated into various other tabloids, and then MTV took it up and it was on their hourly news bulletin. Then American newspapers started ringing up and we hadn't even sold any records in America at that stage! The problem was that Mark's dad was a news agent, so all these people were going into his shop, buying the paper and reading about his lad. People really do believe this sort of stuff, they think it's true if it's written down, so we had to kill that story off. The point is if you have a rock 'n' roll story, something a bit controversial, then it is really easy to get press.'

It is worth remembering here when talking about press that A&R people do read Melody Maker and NME, so if you are in there, especially if it is on a regular basis, then that will really help the buzz. The whole point to all of this self-publicity is not solely to get people to your gigs, it is part and parcel of creating, maintaining and building a 'buzz' in the industry, with a view to getting a record deal.

Bring to the boil

The creation of this buzz has led you and your band up to a boiling point of interest within the industry. There could even be several labels offering you a contract. When one label offers a deal to a band there is often a reaction from other labels who fear they may be missing out on something. A&R guys who have been sitting on the fence up to this stage may decide to commit to a firm offer if it looks like another label are going to sign you up. No one in the industry wants to be the guy who passed on the 'next big thing'. When the 'buzz' reaches a crescendo, it will quite often result in a 'bidding war', when labels try to out-bid each other by raising their advances.

At this point a band really needs a good manager to sort out the deals and pick the one that will be most advantageous for the band in the long run, regardless of whom is offering the biggest advance. However some bands leave this scenario bubbling away for too long – it is crucial not to allow your buzz to 'over boil' or die down. A hot property can quickly become yesterday's 'nearly made its' and the 'buzz' will transfer seamlessly from you to another band. Imagine creating your buzz up to fever pitch, labels want you, the press are championing you, the gigs are full but you leave it too long to sign

TIP

Strike while the iron is hot. Create the buzz, lead up to the point of doing a record deal...and then do it!

the deal, and do a couple of below par gigs. Suddenly one company loses interest and, in the same way as the stock market behaves, there is a lack of confidence, the buzz boils off and the other companies turn their attentions to one of your rivals. Don't let it happen! Read the signs carefully, make sure your manager can cope and then do the deal.

Record companies

*N*ot all record labels and record deals are created equal. In fact any one of us could record a demo on a four track and pass round a few tapes to our friends and call ourselves a 'record label'. There are hundreds of small, local concerns that are run by enthusiasts all over the country. For the next stage in our careers these tiny labels will not be particularly useful to us, we will need to do a deal with an organisation with enough clout to get our records into the shops.

There are two types of record company: independents and majors, and there are pros and cons associated with doing both kinds of deal. Major or Indie label, it is an often repeated (and true) expression in the business that the first 5000 sales are the hardest to achieve.

Independent labels

An independent is so-called because it is independent from its larger cousin the major labels. The major labels are the huge household names, massive corporations like Sony, EMI etc. Indie labels come in all shapes and sizes from tiny backroom offices pressing small quantities of minority interest works to labels like Creation or Mute with international, million selling artists on their rosters, and budgets that equal the majors. Here is a typical indie label set up based on a small company called Cottage Industry.

Cottage Industry has two directors. They put up the finance, take the financial risk and own the company. As directors they have ultimate say in all financial decisions such as who gets signed and what the budget is for any one act's album. There is a Head of International Business who not only looks after import and export deals and licensing but also doubles as an A&R man. The last member of staff is an office manager who also deals with press, booking studios, artwork, and ads and also doubles as an A&R man.

The whole lean operation is run from a prefab on an industrial estate in Nottingham. In spite of its modest size Cottage Industry is potentially a good label for a band to launch their career from because the label has the power to get product into the shops due to its relationship with a distribution company called Total.

Distribution

The record company is responsible for producing a finished product. Because they take the financial risk and put up a considerable investment the record company will own the rights to the recorded work. Having produced an album or single an independent record company will do a deal with a distributor who will actually get the record into the shops. Two distributors for independent product in the UK are Vital and Pinnacle. The major labels are large enough to look after their own distribution. An independent label that hopes to break a new act will have to convince the distributor to take a risk and put a couple of thousand units into the shops. Neither band, label nor distributor will be happy if those units, sold into the shops on sale or return, come back unsold six months down the line. For this reason the distributors will be cautious about

Distribution – it's no good producing the greatest album in pop history if no one can get their hands on it!

handling product from new artists and there will be many acts all vying for national distribution at the same time. It is the job of the distribution company to try and pick the acts that will sell from the ones whose products will sit on the shelf. Small labels will try and present a good case to the distributor, and if the band has profile in the press, a buzz in the industry and is out on the road it will be possible to present a game plan to the distributor that makes sense. National press coupled with a national tour and some great songs will be enough to convince the distributor to take a punt on putting a few thousand units out into the shops. Of course at this stage you will be looking at achieving a presence in the small specialist independent shops, and until your act is selling larger quantities it will be difficult to get your product into the chains or the high street.

Pros and cons of an indie deal

Advantages

The biggest plus of signing to an indie label is credibility. Both the public and the press respond positively to an act that is seen to be 'the real thing'. Some sections of the market are extremely suspicious if they feel an act has been manufactured by a major label, and find the major's slick, corporate approach distasteful. The UK press will often give an indie outfit a much easier ride if they feel they are 'struggling for their art' than an act who have signed to a major.

Life on an indie label – Pulkas get heard on Earache records

The initial 5000 sales are, if not easier to achieve on an indie, certainly cheaper. The lean, stripped down, approach makes it less expensive to deal in small quantities of product. There will be less people working on the project and the indies are set up to deal with the network of specialist shops around the country, whereas the majors are much more at home talking to Woolworth's or HMV about orders in the tens of thousands of units.

Another possible advantage of an independent label is the economics of the actual record deal. A typical major label deal will give the artist a royalty of between 12 to 18 per cent of the gross dealer price. Some indie labels offer a 'shared costs' arrangement with a royalty rate as high as 50 per cent of the gross. In any event most Indies are more flexible and are more likely to negotiate than the majors.

Many artists move to a major label later in their careers having established themselves on an indie. This can work very well. The smaller label can do well out of the arrangement if they are left with a back catalogue which sells well when the band goes on to success on a large scale later on. The major has inherited an act that already has a fan base and whose records may chart even without airplay. Much of the groundwork has already been put in place and the major has so much more to work with than a band who have to be broken from scratch.

Disadvantages

The big drawback of most indie labels is the lack of financial clout. Bruce Dickinson describes the different experiences of being on a major label and an independent.

'When we were recording for Cottage Industry (small indie) our album budget was £4000 and we spent about £500 on the sleeve. On Polydor the album budget was up to £200,000 and I dread to think how much we spent on the sleeves. If I can illustrate one of the differences between a major and an indie it would be this: with Polydor we would have a meeting with one of the marketing guys and our manager to discuss ideas for the sleeve. Everyone would chip in and we'd finally settle on an idea that *nobody disliked*. One of our albums was called 'Jam' and it was decided by committee that we would have a woman's body covered in jam and a couple of wasps would be buzzing round her (this was supposed to symbolise something or other and seemed like a very cool idea at the time). The marketing guy then booked a photographer. When you're on a major you don't mess about with the local paper's photographer you book a serious professional who shoots famous people day in day out and is very expensive. He probably costs upwards of £3000 a day. Our photographer also booked a top model (also expensive) to be covered in jam and photographed. We did the session twice to get the desired effect and the wasps were superimposed, using a computer, by the graphic designer (again – very expensive) who also arranged the lettering. We finally came up with an incredibly expensive sleeve, but there was a problem. You could tell that there was a woman's body under the jam and if you looked very closely you could nearly see a nipple. The marketing department was worried that WH Smith might notice and not stock the record so the graphic designer was hired to mess about with the cover so that the model couldn't be seen. We now had the typical major label sleeve; bland enough for no one to dislike it too much, and no reason for any one to get offended over it and very, very expensive.

On Cottage Industry we had a record called 'Man and Goat Alike' we shot the sleeve ourselves. It was a shot of a goat we found in a field and the budget was probably fifty quid. I like that sleeve much better than many of the expensive ones.'

Major labels

A major label is a huge corporation. There are four main players in the game – Universal (formerly Polygram), Sony, the now amalgamated EMI and Warners, and BMG – each with several related offshoot companies. Universal for example is the parent company to the following labels: Polydor, London, Mercury, A&M, Island and Go-Discs. All these companies are large organisations with several departments and many staff. Each label will have the following departments: Legal, Accounts, A&R, Marketing, Promotions and International. From an artist's point of view a major can be an awesome machine, which has the capability to

Mainstream – play for high stakes on a major label

break acts and co-ordinate international artist's campaigns. Unfortunately there are so many cogs in the system that it is a difficult operation to control. In some cases the major's performances can be likened more to ailing dinosaurs than the powerful corporate machines that they are set up to be.

Structure

The four departments that concern us as artists are A&R, Promotions, Marketing, and International. In this book we will simply give a brief overview of what each department does and how this affects the act.

A&R

INFO

For more detail on how record companies operate, refer to another book in this series – *Set Up Your Own Record Label.*

A&R is an outdated term that originated in the days when songwriters wrote songs for artists who performed other people's work. In the past an A&R man would try to link the right song with the right artist. If he got the combination right then the record company would have a hit record and the publishing company would sell the song on sheet music. In the modern industry these skills are, to a large extent, outdated as most artists write their own material. The A&R person now is responsible for finding and developing new talent. The process of A&R does not stop when a band is signed. An A&R person will help you choose a producer or studio and will also tell you if he doesn't think that your material is good enough. A good relationship with a skilled A&R person is the cornerstone of many an artist's career.

Promotions

This department has the unenviable task of dealing with press, TV and radio. A hit record in the UK still relies very heavily on Radio 1. Radio 1 has a 'playlist meeting' every Thursday morning when the new releases are discussed and the playlist tracks decided for the week. A placing on the A list guarantees a play on every daytime show and invariably helps a record become a hit. This department services MTV and other TV and Video opportunities. A press officer will monitor and create press for the acts under his care.

Marketing

This department will help co-ordinate a campaign and will oversee the retail end as well as booking adverts, running competitions, organising poster campaigns, designing artwork etc. The marketing department also designs the formats for a single release. Formats are the various mediums that a single is released in. A cassette might be one format for example and a CD another. The UK chart system currently allows four formats, and their design and the timing of their release, can affect the chart placing of the single drastically. Some of the more creative format designs have featured: 3 inch CDs, Vinyl 12 inch picture discs, Wooden Boxes, Leather pouches, Holograms, flashing lights – there has even been a CD released inside a vacuum cleaner bag!

International

The International department is responsible for imported product in the UK and also creating opportunities for international sales for domestic product. An international campaign must be carefully co-ordinated and an international hit single must be planned in advance. For example, a track that is receiving heavy rotation on MTV must be available to buy in the shops for it to be a hit all round Europe.

The pros and cons of a major label deal

Advantages

The first advantage is pretty obvious – majors generally have a lot more money to spend than indies. This means they can afford to be generous with budgets for recording, promotions, formats, videos and advances. Majors have much more clout at retail and can pull favours in order to get relatively unknown acts into the high street shops. The odds of an act achieving substantial success are increased because there are so many more resources available to the artist on a major.

Disadvantages

Because there are more processes and people involved there are more things to go wrong. It only takes a breakdown of communication between two departments to completely hamstring an act's single or album release. There is generally much less artistic freedom on a major and you will be forced to consider many commercial factors when making decisions about the direction of the project. The biggest drawback however is the fact that the royalty rate on a major label deal is typically 12 – 18 per cent of the gross dealer price of a CD. This means that if the dealer price (the price that the shops buy in the CD at) is £7.25 the artist will receive around £1 (give or take a few pence either side depending on the rate). If that were not bad enough the artist has to pay all the recording costs and advances back out of these meagre royalties. The 'debt' to the label will remain unrecouped until the band has sold enough units to pay back the costs. At that point in theory the band will earn royalties. In reality an album may cost £200,000 to produce and the advance may be £150,000. A gold album in the UK is only 100,000 units so if you do your maths you will realise that it will take international success on a large scale to recoup the debt. Most bands, even those with hit records, are locked into a cycle of debt, with each advance and album increasing the debt. Check out the pie chart at the end of this chapter for a breakdown of the costs on a full price major label album.

Having a hit record

Once a band is signed to a major they face enormous pressure to deliver a hit single. Hit singles are how a label markets an album. Profits on single sales are negligible at best and many singles are regarded as loss leaders, the loss being hopefully offset against the profits on the resulting album sales. Historically some bands have refused to play the marketing game and not released singles. Today however, even left field bands have to chart somehow to stand a chance of long term survival.

Publishing companies

As well as the royalties due to the band on their recorded work there is another set of royalties due to the writers of the songs. These royalties are collected and distributed by the publishing company. Publishing companies come in all shapes and sizes and all the major labels have offshoot publishing companies.

By law a fixed percentage of royalties on any record sale go to the writer of the song. These royalties are called mechanicals. A songwriter can do a deal with the publisher and receive an advance on future royalties. The publisher is then obliged to physically collect the royalties due to the writer and also 'maximise the potential of the song' by working towards its use in any area that it would earn money for the writer, such as: film, video games, advertisements etc. The publisher will also publish songs as sheet music.

Royalties are also paid to the writer after every play on radio, TV, juke box, lift or supermarket intercom. There royalties are collected by the PRS (Performing Right Society) who hold onto the money for six months, keeping the interest, in return for collecting it. A big international hit can generate several hundred thousand pounds for the writer within a few weeks.

The publisher typically keeps 20 per cent of the royalties collected. An advance on a publishing deal can be anything from nothing to well over a million pounds. A typical advance for a band on a major label would be around £50-100,000. Some bands sign a publishing deal before a record deal, and although the advance is likely to be smaller, the publisher is then obliged to try and get a record deal for the act.

The fact that there are additional royalties available to the songwriters can cause all kinds of problems within the band. Some bands choose to deal with this by sharing out the royalties equally between the various members of the project. In other bands there is an obvious difference between the lifestyles of the main songwriters and the other band members. For this reason it is important to decide who has written a song as soon as possible after its composition.

Legally the writer of the song is defined as the writer of the top line melody and the lyrics. Morally however, most reasonable people would agree that some instrumental parts and drum grooves are central to the composition. The question is 'where does arrangement stop and composition start?' because it is certainly true to say that just turning up and putting some parts around someone else's tune is not 'writing'. The writers of the tune are those who the band decide have contributed to the creation of the piece. Some writers have been credited just because they happened to be in the room at the time a song was written. Song writing is a mysterious process and who is to say that those individuals did not contribute to the atmosphere that allowed that song to be born.

The song is registered with the publishing company before a record is released. It is perfectly possible to break down the writing credits using a percentage system. The writer of the lyrics and melody might get 50 per cent, the writer of the riffs and chord sequence 30 per cent and the guy who came up with the hooky drum groove might get the remaining 20 per cent. This percentage is then registered with the publisher who distributes the royalties accordingly. Problems start when the band cannot agree who has written the track. This is why it is easier to decide who is responsible for what the same day the song is written. It can be difficult to recall a writing session a few weeks down the line and people's memories can become very selective when there are large quantities of money at stake.

Income and expenses for the performing artist

As we have discovered, getting a record deal doesn't automatically mean that you are going to earn a huge amount from the record company itself. But if you are not going to be receiving royalties until your album goes double platinum, how on earth are you going to survive on the modest advance you receive every time you deliver an album. Well the good news is that you don't need to rely on this alone, because you can make money from a variety of sources. The trick is to know what is going on and to take an active part in all financial matters. This way you can be involved in maximising the returns and deciding what to do with the revenue that you have generated.

Income

The first pie chart displays the possible distribution of income from various sources for a typical band. Of course each individual will get a different split of the income and no two bands have exactly the same financial situation, but this diagram will give you a rough idea of a 'typical' income for a moderately successful band.

Potential Income for the performing artist. NB. All percentages are approximate and will vary depending on a band's individual circumstances.

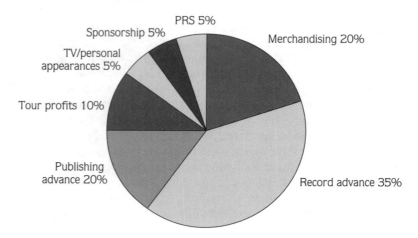

In addition there will be royalties on record sales at 12-18 per cent on retail unit price after advances and recording costs are paid back to the record company, plus mechanical royalties to songwriter paid from the record company to the artist via the MCPS (Mechanical Copyright Protection Society) and the publisher. If the writer has taken an advance this will have to be paid back before any royalties come through (minus 20 per cent or so which the publisher keeps and another 20 per cent which the manager commissions).

Expenses

The second pie chart shows how a band might choose to spend the money. N.B. Gear refers to musical equipment, not drugs!

These figures do not include any touring losses incurred through inaccurate budgeting, and support tours not funded by the record company.

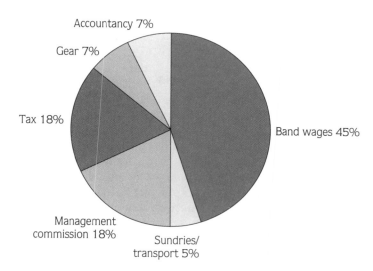

Accountancy 7%

Gear 7%

Tax 18%

Management commission 18%

Sundries/ transport 5%

Band wages 45%

Potential expenses for the performing artist

Breakdown of album costs

The final chart shows exactly why you need to plan to earn from other areas as well as record sales. Also check out what happens to the money you shell out for a full price CD. Don't forget you have to pay back your advances and recording costs out of your 6.5% artist share.

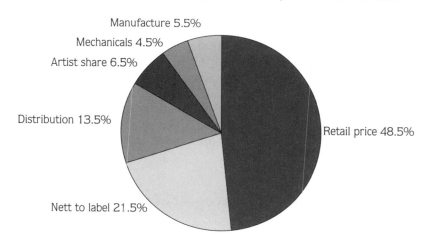

Manufacture 5.5%

Mechanicals 4.5%

Artist share 6.5%

Distribution 13.5%

Nett to label 21.5%

Retail price 48.5%

Breakdown cost of full price album with typical UK major label
Gross dealer price = 51.5%
Retail mark up = 48.5%

Record deals over the internet

As well as the traditional view of how records can be made and sold, it is also rather important that we address future technological developments in the industry. There is a very real possibility that the traditional medium of selling musical product will be, if not superseded, seriously challenged by forward thinking companies selling and marketing product over the internet. Perhaps we should begin by asking ourselves some basic questions.

How do people buy music over the internet already?

Music can be downloaded over the internet in a variety of formats. The most popular by far is the MP3 file. This is a digital format offering near CD quality in a compact file size. To receive this information you will need: a computer, a modem (a device which allows your computer to link to the internet), and an MP3 player of some description (this could be a piece of software on your computer or an external piece of hardware that looks a bit like a walkman). Most MP3 files on the Net are pirate versions of commercial recordings and midi files of karoake versions of popular tunes. Again much of this is unregulated and available free with no royalties being paid to the writers or performers of the pieces. However, this is likely to change as major record companies and publishers are working on ways to protect files with codes so that the copyright can be protected.

Many small artists have been using the internet as a marketing tool and selling their product mail order, as a direct result, for years. One of the first record companies actually selling on the net using MP3 files was peoplesound.com. Several other similar organisations now exist signing unsigned bands, sometimes even offering a small advance and marketing their product, selling it and giving the artist a 50% royalty on the full retail price of the product. On the face of it this is a great deal especially when the artist can terminate the arrangement easily if they wish to enter into an exclusive arrangement with a major label. Only time will tell how effective these labels will be in attracting significant sales for their acts. mp3.com allows free downloads of individual tracks and is used as a marketing tool by labels and unsigned bands alike. The idea is that surfers will download one track free, and then buy the album if they like it. The company also makes money by selling advertising space on the site.

What are the future developments likely to be?

Of course the big record companies are extremely active in the development of their own interests on the internet (the words 'headless' and 'chicken' come to mind). One of the major advances of recent times has been the merger of EMI with Time Warner and America On Line (The ISP or internet service provider). For the first time we have a massive music conglomerate with huge and direct internet links. This makes the move towards a future where all major label product will be available over the net inevitable. High street chain stores are acutely aware of their vulnerability (imagine the savings that a company could make by avoiding distribution and retail costs), and are trying to get some kind of commitment from the major labels to secure their future. Musicians around the

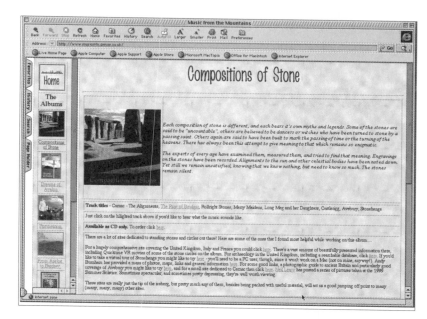

The website for the small label Music from the Mountains – simple but effective

globe are watching and waiting to see how this will all pan out, and of course the smart acts are developing their own band homepages (home produced web pages). Some established bands are selling all kinds of products through their website, and directly reaching a much larger percentage of their fanbase than they were ever able to before.

How do I produce a Website for my band?

Web design is a potentially complex (and lucrative) business so we suggest that you research this subject in depth. However it is relatively simple to set up a basic homepage and there is plenty of help out there. If you go on to the internet and search for say 'homepage design', you will be able to find plenty of sites which will take you through the process. It is important to try and get a great and simple name for your website. If you can get **thenameofyourband.com** then you are half way there. The other half is ensuring that people actually come to your site, have a good look and maybe even buy something. The best way to get potential fans surfing through your site is to organise links from other, associated sites and get your site onto all the big search engines. This will mean, for example, that when someone types 'indie rock' into their search engine, your site is one of the sites that appears. Simple!

However if you are a technophobe, you may need to become friendly with a computer nerdy type who, in return for basking in the reflected glory of your rock star status, will design a site for you so long as you promise to help get him a girlfriend.

6 ★ *People power*

TIP

*I*f an A&R person hears of your band, comes to see you at a gig and it happens to be the one where you have made no effort to get fans along, they are going to be rather unimpressed and probably walk away without making any contact with you. This is the most crucial stage in your career plan, fans must come to see the band on a regular basis.

*N*ow that your band has successfully developed a buzz, not only in the local area but also in London, it is time to consider ways of holding on to the fan base that has been created and extending it. This will ensure that whereever your band does a gig at least some people will come, and the buzz will grow even more prior to doing a record deal.

So you're doing some local gigs, some London gigs and some national gigs and people like what they are hearing and enjoy what they are seeing. Now is the time to make the most of what you have built so far, now is the time to create that fan base. This is a solid foundation that can be relied upon to buy the products, i.e. tapes or records, T-shirts or posters, and to turn up at the ever more important gigs.

Compiling a database

Be organised about this because a database is the best way to ensure that your fan base knows what you are up to and where you are playing. It could be a card filing system if you do not have access to a computer, but somehow you need to collect the names and addresses of as many people as possible who are into the band, and even those who have shown only a passing interest, in order to start your fan club. This way you can have regular contact with your fan base via mail shots. Obviously a computer is a far more organised and simple method of controlling a database, because even the simplest machine will possess a database system or a mail merge facility.

If you have, for example, Windows '95 then the Office facility contains a program called Access which is specifically for setting up a database, allowing you to extend and customise your fan base information at your leisure. It may also be a good idea to invest in a franking machine which is a good way of sending large amounts of post without having to lick a lot of stamps. The old machines have to be fed with tokens that can be bought from the post office, but the newer ones can be loaded electronically by credit card.

Make contact, but beware

In order to build a database you will need to collect the information from your fans in the first place, and the easiest way to do this initially is to prepare a postcard that can be handed out at your gigs. This will allow people who want to know more about the band to either fill them in there and then with their details, or to take them home and then send them to you by post at their leisure. However as the band gets bigger you do not want your personal address going out to everybody and anybody. This may sound slightly paranoid but it is a statement of fact that even a band that is only large on a local scale can attract some strange or obsessive fans.

TIP

Set up a PO Box at your local post office, and all your band post can go to a safe address

One example of this was of a band called Headnoise in the Guildford area who had quite a large following and a mailing list card that gave the home address of the singer. All went well for the band for a while using this system, and then the singer began to receive letters written with cut-out newspaper. These letters were not necessarily of a threatening nature on the surface, but they did suggest that he was being followed around because the fan was infatuated with him having seen him at all the band's gigs.

While nothing ever actually physically happened to the singer, it did mean that he had to move house to ensure his safety. Gigs also became something of a nightmare for him, wondering if the obsessive fan was in the audience and worrying about what they might do, if anything. So you can see the immediate benefits of setting up a Post Office Box which is very simple to organise at your local post office, costs about £52 per year and means all your band post can go to a safe address where you can pick it up on a weekly basis. This is also about the time that you can think about starting up a small mail order business for any band products.

In the club

Once you have a database together, even if it only consists of a hundred names and addresses, it is an idea to consider setting up a fan club to make your following official. At such an early stage in your career it is unwise to attempt to charge your fans to become members, because what you are looking for is sheer weight of numbers. So make it a free service consisting of a quarterly newsletter containing some inside information about the band. It could be entertaining in style with a family atmosphere about it, you could give members the opportunity to receive tracks or demos that have not been put into the public domain, and they would be exclusive to the fan club members. However do not forget that if the band becomes successful, these demos could become sought after, so make sure that they are not too rough!

It is important that the fan club contains a vibe, the members should feel like they are part of a little scene, that the band is eventually going to be successful and that they were there from the start. By doing this you will be building the perception that, from the fans point of view, it is a good idea to be in on this. Again this is a little bit of hype and psychology, you need to get your fans thinking that they do not want to miss out on what could be the next big thing. But remember if you do not believe some of it yourself, then why are you bothering?

Use them or lose them

After a while even a small band should have put together a database of between two to three thousand people, especially after a few reasonable gigs, but the effort required to build the database and the database itself become useless if you do not then take advantage of it. Imagine how many small bands there are who have been organised enough to create a database, but not motivated enough to bother using it. Phrases like 'it's too much like hard work' or 'it's too expensive' become commonplace and then bands wonder why no one knows about their gigs.

Be organised and motivated, every time you do a gig in a certain area do a mail shot to all the fans on your database that live in and around that area. How? If you are using a computer make sure that you file people's information away using their area or region as a key word filter. Then when it comes to finding all your fans in, say, the Wolverhampton area, you use Wolverhampton and Birmingham as your filters to access all the addresses in those areas. The database program will then find all the appropriate addresses and prepare them for printing, either onto envelopes or sticky labels.

If you want to get really organised, then consider how most businesses categorise their customers into age and sex as well as how many times those customers have used their services. While this might sound a little excessive remember that you are selling a product, and therefore it is important to know your market and who is buying that product, so you can begin to target that category of person more effectively. You must try to give people what they want, not what you think they want.

The fan club

To understand fan clubs and the way they work it is a good idea to study successful ones. One man who understands fan clubs more than most is Mike Hrano who represents, and is the official international fan club operator for: Boyzone, Chris De Burgh, East 17, Gary Barlow, Mark Owen, Menswear, Pet Shop Boys, Peter Andre, Roachford and Status Quo. Mike's previous clients include Seal, Sonia, Bros., Big Fun, Whigfield and The Christians, to name a few. So the first question must be, what is a fan club and why should a band set one up?

'A fan club is the bridge between the artist and the supporter, i.e. the fan. The fan club ought to give the fans an exclusive access and involvement with the artist. Obviously there is an ulterior motive here, because what the switched on artist wants to do is take care of the fans who in turn take care of their career, and make them rich and famous.

There are two types of fan and two types of fan club. The fan clubs that I run are fan clubs that involve a payment being made for the privilege, if you like, of that exclusivity and that additional information that nobody else can get. So these are people who haven't just said 'we are fans', they have paid money to nail their colours to the mast, they are the hard-core. The other fans are people who have written into the fan club but ultimately have decided they don't want to join. They then go on a wider database so that if we wanted to mail people about a new single, if it was just a non-exclusive mailing, then we would add this onto the fan club's mailing list.'

What has to be pointed out at this juncture is the huge difference between a fan club and what it does for its members, and enclosure cards. Enclosure cards are the freepost cards that record companies place inside compact discs that are returnable for more information about a band or an act. This is marketing, it is saying 'you have bought the record, can we give you further information'. This 'further information' arrives in the form of an inducement to buy, i.e. buy the new single because they want it to enter the charts, buy the album, come and see the band on tour or buy the video. This is not what fan clubs are about. Fans are there to be serviced, not used purely to to enhance the position of any particular artist and make money for the record company. Consider it this way, if the only time a band's record company gets in contact with you is to sell you the latest product, this cannot be considered as a service to the fan, i.e. you. What fan clubs do is give you the option to buy these and many other things, but if you do not want them they will continue to send you the information that you require without the hard sell.

A large percentage of the people who work for record companies appear to vaguely understand the power of marketing, therefore they understand that when they launch a band an enclosure card is a good way of accessing and building a database of fans who support that band. However what tends to happen in this situation is that the band reaches a certain level of success and suddenly their database becomes non-cost effective. They will be able to fund the first 25,000 enquiries, but when it grows to 175,000, and the band is becoming self-sufficiently successful, the record company feel that they no longer need, or can afford, to call upon the support of those early fans, and ultimately they stop contacting anybody. The most important feature of this situation is ensuring that you take care of every single fan that has shown physical support for your band, because the second that you believe that you can succeed without sending out information to your original fan base, you will have 25,000 fans who feel that they have been urinated upon.

TIP

If a band loses its solid base of support, then when things start to go badly there will be no one there to help.

Three steps to fan club heaven

Step 1 VFM
The key to any successful fan club is *value for money*. This means the right kind of service and the right kind of information being provided for the fan.

Step 2 Reliability
You must also be able to deliver to people the information or the goods that you have taken their money for. There are hundreds of horror stories about fan clubs that started off with the best intentions in the world, and also the worst intentions, and gone bust. You must have the ability to deliver what you promise.

Step 3 Exclusivity
Members should be able to get a service from a fan club that non-members are not entitled to.

Day-to-day

It is a good idea at this point to have a closer look at how a professional fan club is run on a regular basis. Obviously this may not appear to be important at this particular moment in your career, but imagine how important it will be when you become successful.

The first point to remember about fan clubs, as with all aspects of becoming successful, is time management. When a band becomes successful the volume of mail that it receives is quite frightening, so it is important to be disciplined and work in cycles on a week by week basis. Mike Hrano described his working practices,

'The mail is picked up from the sorting offices where we have PO addresses every Tuesday and Friday, the mail is then opened and sorted into several distinct piles. There will be people who want information about the fan club who automatically go onto our database which allows us to send them an application form. There is another batch of returned application forms with money or returned merchandising order forms with money, all that money is then banked. When all the cheques have cleared, because people bounce cheques on us all the time, they are put into the system and we will call up their files on the database and put an x in their box, which tells us they're a member. With the merchandising orders it's the same, once the cheques have cleared they will be dispatched. We may also be running different forms of post like competitions or pen pals, and these are all individually sorted. If gifts have been sent they will be passed onto the band. We also receive, for want of a better phrase, sob stories. There will be people with leukaemia, cerebral palsy, terrible illnesses, who will be requesting backstage passes or meetings or signed photographs. I pass those over to the management because that's not my court, it's not for me to decide.

Then within the context of each week there will be mailings to be prepared, news letters to be written, interviews to be done. I would say that, across the board of the acts that I'm working with, at least every month I've got an interview with Boyzone or Peter Andre or Status Quo. Once that's all done, we'll have a mail shot – it's a lot of stuff.

Just sorting the cheques out can be a day's work, and when I'm walking into a bank with a bunch of cheques, bound together by an elastic band that's the size of a brick, I can barely get them through the gap that allows you to give them to the cashier. It can be seriously big business!'

From this outline it is easy to see just how organised you must be, because each enquiry or application needs to treated individually. Attention to detail is uppermost in this form of operation, simply because each person that sends in a letter or an application form expects to receive a one-on-one service. This is as close as most fans will get to their beloved artist, so make it count. Also notice that if a fan club is run properly, and therefore successfully, it can generate a large amount of money.

... and what size would you like

When it comes to selling merchandise it is important to remember
that we live in an integrated capitalist society. What does this
mean? Basically it means that everybody is in business to provide a
service at a profit, and our capitalist culture is based upon this
simple tenet. When it comes to selling merchandise it is possible to
give value for money to your fans and still make a profit. For
example, it is perceived by the public that £11 for a T-shirt that
carries the official logo and artwork of their chosen band or artist,
is good value for money. However you can guarantee that the fan
club is not paying £11 for the shirt to be produced, indeed they will
be making a healthy profit margin on the garment.

So who is supported by that profit margin? It is not just for the
fan club or the band or the management to make money, it is there
to create wealth within the concept of the fan club in order for it to
be self-sufficient and be able to sustain itself. The fan club makes
money to enable it to continue to provide a service. What the public
do not necessarily understand is that when they go to Wembley
Arena for a concert and a T-shirt costs £15, it is more expensive
because Wembley Arena take 25 per cent of the gross price of the
shirt just for allowing a band to sell it there. Add to this the various
other expenses such as transportation costs and this drives the
price of the merchandise way beyond that original profit margin.
However this urge for profit is not always totally beneficial, as Mike
Hrano describes:

> 'I do apply an equation to merchandising, and sometimes that
> equation doesn't allow me a profit because it is not just about
> profit, it's about service. So if I've got a demand for, say, a Gary
> Barlow poster that doesn't ostensibly make me any money, if the
> demand is there and people want to buy it and I can cover my
> costs, pay for my staff, pay for the postage and packing and allow
> x amount of people to have that poster that they really want,
> without me making money then I will do that too, because that is a
> service.'

When it comes to what sort of merchandise can be sold the list is
endless and is really only defined by imagination and finance. For
the major bands the financial side is not so much of a criterion, it
could be East 17 jogging trousers or Boyzone rucksacks, Status Quo
jackets or Spice Girls dresses, the list is endless. However the most
important piece of merchandise for any band or artist is the good
old T-shirt. These days the traditional T-shirt has expanded to
accommodate other styles such as the skinny rib T-shirt and ribbed
T-shirts with V necks. These are motivated by fashion so it is a good
idea to keep an eye on these trends, because not everybody will
wear a traditional style shirt, but you may be able to tickle their
fancy with something a little different.

Fanzines – Boyzone know the importance of looking after a loyal fanbase

Ultimately what a T-shirt says uncategorically is 'I like this act, look at me, this is the band I support'. Think of the amount of Metallica T-shirts that can be seen in your local town on a Saturday afternoon, now try and imagine that amount of people wearing your band's T-shirt. That is a serious amount of unbridled support and an awesome amount of advertising and promotion.

The psychology of the 'fan'

This is a good time to analyse the point mentioned earlier that when a band becomes successful and holds some form of celebrity status, even if that success is based solely in their home town, it can cause problems. This success can suddenly make even the most unattractive or average looking band members extremely attractive to certain members of the opposite, or the same, sex. The term 'fan' was originally derived from the word fanatic and is generally used to describe any person who feels an ideological or identity link with another's appearance or work, i.e. music and musical performances. However there is a definite difference in the reactions between the dusty professor who has spent his life revelling in the works of Charles Dickens (although it is possible that at one time the professor may well have wished for the opportunity to be able to meet Dickens), and the legendary Sixties groupies the Plaster

Blur inspired their fair share of female adulation

Casters who used dental plaster to make casts of their rock hero's genitals.

In the past, pop music fans have been subjected to intellectual damnation by an elitist group of Marxist cultural theorists and sociologists. The Marxist Theodor Adorno had this to say on the subject of pop fans,

> 'In general they are intoxicated by the fame. What is important to them is the sense of belonging as such, identification, without paying particular attention to its content. Merely to be carried away by anything at all, to have something of their own, compensates for their impoverished and barren existence.'[1]

Many writings on the subject of fans tend to focus in on the idea of the 'pathological fan' who has been divided into two categories: the obsessed loner who is involved in an 'intense fantasy relationship with a celebrity figure', which can lead to threatening or dangerous behaviour. The second category are the 'frenzied or hysterical members of a crowd', who scream or shout at their idols en masse.

Of course this form of categorisation normally comes from so-called academics who, due to their lack of involvement in a particular form of entertainment, feel they are able to cast a

1 For more on this subject, check out *Sound Effects: Youth, Leisure, and the politics of rock 'n' roll* by Simon Frith (1983).

patronising eye over a subject that they know little about and understand even less. There are dangerous individuals like Mark David Chapman who killed John Lennon, but these psychologically deranged people exist in all walks of life and their actions are not necessarily motivated directly by their victims. In this well documented case Chapman was apparently driven to kill Lennon after reading J.D. Salinger's book *The Catcher In The Rye*. And there are hordes who throng round their heroes screaming and crying, but this does not make them automatically less intelligent or less rational people than those who do not act this way.

Remember also that fans possess significant control over the music industry. Popular music is only popular because people buy it, and what the public buys is not controlled by anyone. Record companies cannot market a band into being successful, the marketing will help but ultimately the public will buy what they like. The outcome of this is that the music industry tends to respond to public musical taste rather than direct it. Ultimately, therefore, the most important and the most influential sector of the music business is the fan, without the fan the music business could not, and would not, exist. However ...

Ooh, I say

Fans, and especially female fans, have become a part of rock folklore. Stories of groupies fill the biographies of all the big bands with sordid acts of sexual degradation and excess, and these women have been vilified for their actions from most corners. Whatever people may think or say, groupies have been, and will remain, a part of the rock musician's experience. Jenny, a groupie who started the fanzine 'Slapper', described her feelings towards other groupies and her own ideals in The Observer newspaper,

'I suddenly realised that these were amazing women. They use their initiative, they get things free, they have the most amazing lifestyles. People who think it's degrading are just ignorant. Talent is just as good a criterion for choosing sexual partners as any other, isn't it? You have a fantastic time, room service, free booze and great no-strings sex with incredibly talented people. Excuse me, but isn't that what rock's meant to be about? Groupies aren't the pariahs of rock 'n' roll, they're its lifeblood. These are grown men, no one's forcing them into bed are they? They can always say no. AIDs? Use a condom, what's the problem?' [2]

An example of how groupies can conduct themselves is supplied by a couple of women who went under the moniker of the 'Elastic Fantastic Girls'. They were based in and around the Manchester

2 For more about this read *Popular Music and Society* by Brian Longhurst (1995).

area, but covered a number of the northern venues, where they would go to gigs and then work their way into the backstage area afterwards. The girls, who cannot be named for legal reasons, would then choose a member of the band and make their intentions clearly known. They would accompany the band member back to his hotel room and there they would indulge in various sexual activities, that would culminate in them taking large elastic bands out of a case and wrapping the bands around themselves and the band member in such a way as to ensure that while the elastic bands were flexible enough to get into a rhythm, there was no way of escape until the girls had finished. Some band members found the experience invigorating, others however did not.

Obviously it is extremely important here to stress that there is a vast difference between groupies, who have a history of direct sexual involvement between themselves and the bands, and groups of screaming teenage fans at a Boyzone concert, who are part of a cultural display and an integral part of pop music heritage that can be traced back to the Beatles. Teenage hysteria and infatuation with boy bands is an accepted phenomenon, and a large percentage of teenage girls, in particular, enjoy this demonstration of early sexuality before they 'grow up', or rather move on to a different plane of support.

Suits you to a T sir 7

W hen it comes to selling merchandise, as has been mentioned before, there are few boundaries, and all bands who have any form of following will, or should, have something that they can sell. There are three reasons for this: firstly it is a good way of raising much needed capital for the band, secondly it can help to raise the profile of a band or artist and thirdly it gives the fan base the opportunity to 'tie their colours to the mast', i.e. it allows fans the opportunity to demonstrate their support for a particular act. When it comes to actually selling goods there are three main outlets where band merchandising can be effectively marketed; retail outlets (like record shops, but this is dependent on the success of the act), fan clubs and gigs. Of course, regardless of what anybody may tell you, the most famous piece of band merchandise by a long, long mile is the inimitable T-shirt.

It's you to a T

Throughout recent rock history the T-shirt has become an icon by which bands have been able to measure their success, not just as a band but by the way that that band has been iconically depicted. One of the most important and pervasive details that a band needs to turn its attention to is not necessarily the name of the band (as music history is littered with successful bands with terrible names) but the design of the band's logo. This can not only make or break

T-shirts – never mind the quality read the slogan!

the success of a T-shirt, but it is also an extremely important part of a band's definition. The hippie era was dominated by the 'Dead Head' image of the Grateful Dead, the late 70's and early 80's were given another reason to be cheerful by the 'Blockhead' logo of Ian Dury and the Blockheads, in the mid to late 80's everyone was wearing Frankie Goes To Hollywood's 'Relax' T-shirts, and the 90's has seen a plethora of superb logo designs including the multi-million selling Metallica T-shirts and the 'crop top' Spice Girls T-shirts. Not only do bands now understand the importance of a good design, many artists themselves now pinpoint their own musical references by wearing other band's T-shirts for live shows and promotional shots.

All of this can only mean one thing; merchandising, and T-shirts in particular, are big business, and there is no one bigger in this country when it comes to T-shirt design, supply and distribution than Bravado International Group. Based in London, Bravado have been at the forefront of merchandising and T-shirt supply for 20 years. Why? Because they work hard at defining exactly who the fans are of the bands that they represent. For example, when they were working with the Spice Girls for a tour, they looked at the age group and dominant sex of the fan base and design the range of merchandise around the potential audience that will turn up to a Spice Girls concert. However even they were surprised by the make up of the audience, as Maria Conroy from Bravado explains:

'We started in Dublin with the Spice Girls and we knew that it was going to be a young audience, but it was still a real surprise to see just how young. The average age in Dublin must have been about five years old, they were tiny. I was sat next to a little baby who was asleep on the chair while the mother was holding hands and dancing with her son and daughter. Honestly it was even more of a surprise than we had anticipated, we had taken a large amount of kids T-shirts because I thought the average age would be about thirteen, so after that gig we had to change the breakdown of the T-shirt sizes for the rest of the concerts. Just because we start off a tour with a range it doesn't mean that it is written in stone, we can chop and change as it goes along.

Really we look at the band, we look at their audience, we look at the album artwork, where they are playing and then we would put a proposal together based on these factors.

Financially with a lot of bands we pay an advance against a royalty which is recoupable, that's a pretty straightforward way of doing it. With other bands we do a split profit deal when we are not really sure how well they are going to do because we don't want to commit to giving them money. This is working more as a partnership, which works really well and most of the time, if the band are happy with a split profit deal, we will continue this partnership for the next tour. Otherwise we would look at giving them an advance which makes it easier for accounting purposes.'

It is very important for a company like Bravado to work with the band or the band's management to ensure that all the designs have been approved before they go on the road. Otherwise once they are on the road, if the shirts are not selling well, it is the company's T-shirt sellers that will get the brunt of the band's disappointment. It is for this very reason that everybody must be happy with the

Buy, buy, buy. T-shirts, records, fan club membership, being a fan is an expensive business

merchandise, because then if the shirts do not sell it is time to go back to the drawing board and try again. Bravado will go as far as to generate ten different designs, send them to the band and allow the band to decide which ones they like the best. Only once they are decided upon will Bravado then do the final artwork for the proofs.

Supplying the big boys

When a company is as successful as Bravado it will be able to work with the bigger acts, supplying shirts that can be seen on every high street. At the moment they are working with acts like Depeche Mode, Iron Maiden, Halloween, The Spice Girls, Motorhead, Page and Plant, Tori Amos, Blur and Paul Weller. Although a large percentage of the bands that Bravado represent at the moment are rock based bands, it is no longer the case that these types of bands are the only successful sellers of T-shirts. The days of seeing solely metal or rock band shirts have past, and this is mainly down to the fact that many shops these days stock large amounts of character licensed shirts, an example being the Bart Simpson 'Eat My Shorts' shirt. There is no getting away from the fact also that pop bands have begun to realise the potential power of the T-shirt and are now dominating the market in certain areas. The pop power moguls are now understanding that the short termism of many teen pop acts can be financially extended by merchandising, so Bravado are now supplying shirts for acts that can be sold by the truckload and thus help compensate for the band's possibly brief existence.

Successful shirts

According to Maria from Bravado, the most successful T-shirt was the Spice Girls shirt with a picture of the girls on the front. Why was this shirt successful? Well it was not because the design was particularly ground breaking or artistically brave, it was purely because there were so many young girls out there who were eager to show support for the act by having their image emblazoned across their shirts. For success through design, however, Maria chose another band:

> 'The Wonderstuff, they always did really well on their merchandise and that was really because they had such a great logo. The shirts were cool and the band were cool, they were one of the few bands that you could literally just put their logo on a shirt and that would be it. You didn't have to mess about adding to it because that would complicate the design, they also had some great artwork as well and we used to go out with loads of different shirts, but it was always the logo shirt. We could do loads of different shirt colours but for about five years, whenever they

toured, we had to have a logo shirt. Their logo just worked brilliantly, it was a perfect example of a logo that you could slap on anything and it worked.

The Little Angels as well, their shirts were excellent because they had the name and they had the 'devil' design, so you could put the devil on the front of a T-shirt, without the logo, and everyone still knew it was the Little Angels. When you can do something like that then you know that you have hit something really successful. It's the same with 'Eddie' from Iron Maiden, you could just put him on the front of a shirt and everybody would know that it was a Maiden shirt.'

This proves the importance of the two things that make up a successful T-shirt; a good logo for the band's name and a good graphic image representation of the band's identity. One of these is extremely important, but both together is a real coup. This is also where it is important for the band to be involved in the process of creating a representation for that band. There is little point in just slapping a picture on the front of a shirt and hoping for the best (unless you are the Spice Girls), the most successful merchandising lines are always the ones where the band are personally involved in the creation. Most bands in this position rarely know what they want, but are certain of what they do not want which can be very frustrating for the designer and goes to demonstrate that the band have not really considered themselves as a defined unit.

Think of it this way; a band has spent a large amount of time coming up with what they believe to be the ultimate name. That name is likely to be with them right the way through their career. Now imagine how much more successful that name could be if it were incorporated into a simple yet striking logo that was good enough to last for the duration of the life of the band, undergoing few changes and ultimately being as recognisable as the name itself. Eventually a name means nothing but the way it is written or depicted becomes everything. Few people look back and think 'Pink Floyd, what a terrible name for a band', what is remembered is the artwork and the album covers. And remember that a band logo will appear on everything that is linked with the band, it will be on the records, tapes and compact discs, on the flyers and posters, on the backdrop, on stickers.

What is a good shirt?

Some T-shirt designs have been supremely unsuccessful and an example of this was an especially tasteless effort from Wet Wet Wet. Normally capable of selling large amounts of merchandise, the Wets decided that they wanted to supply a lycra crop top with 'We ♥ Wets' printed on the front. Unfortunately no one could talk their manager Elliot out of it, and the result is that there are a huge amount of these T-shirts sitting in boxes in a warehouse somewhere in London today.

So what makes a popular T-shirt? Here is a simple fact; Black T-shirts sell better than white T-shirts. Of course this fact really means very little today because of the vast array of different styles that are available at every large concert. When M People went out on tour they were selling the album T-shirt, a photo T-shirt, a logo-graphic shirt, a fitted skinny shirt, a V neck ribbed shirt and an embroidered fleece top. However if you are in a band that is trying to forge a future in music, and you are attempting to design a shirt to sell at gigs for money and a higher profile, it is a good place to start.

Another aspect to a successful shirt, as has been discussed above, is attempting to ensure some form of longevity for it. A good logo and a simple, timeless design will allow your band the opportunity to continue to sell a shirt years after it was originally introduced. Do not make tour shirts if that tour is only going to last five dates, because you will not be able to sell those shirts after the event. Having said that, a limited date shirt can work with a little thought. For example if your band is only playing five dates around England, there is no reason to list only these dates on the shirt, with just a little imagination the band could be playing the Kings Head, Fulham on Monday and The Great Wall of China on Tuesday. By injecting the shirt with a little humour not only does it advertise the real gigs, but it suddenly becomes a more collectable item.

Let's do the deal

Many in the know will advise a band not to sell or give away their merchandising rights as this obviously means that all profits raised go directly to the band, and in the beginning of a band's career this is very important. There will be many occasions in a band's early days when the only money they will make to cover expenses such as new strings or petrol will be from the sale of a few T-shirts at a gig. But once a band is on its way a merchandising deal can help out enormously. Firstly merchandising deals are quite short term, they tend just to last for one tour and after that the band get their rights back. It is not like a recording or publishing deal where a band is giving away its rights for a long period of time.

Secondly, while it is possible to do the merchandising yourself and earn more out of it, it is a large amount of hassle, it is a very specialised area and there is a lot of boot-legging of merchandise that needs to be controlled somehow if you are to make the optimum from your original merchandise. Ultimately it is down to the band and their manager to decide which way is best. With a merchandising deal the band will receive an advance from the merchandising company, but they will have to split the receipts at the end of the tour. Without a merchandising deal the band receives all the profits but has to design, produce, supply and sell the T-shirts, the result of which will ultimately be less profit.

Pounds per head

This is the way a company like Bravado will decide whether or not a band is going to be a viable prospect. It is also a good, and easy, way for a small band to find out whether they are marketing their T-shirts properly. Quite simply you add up how much money was made from the sale of shirts at a gig and then divide it by the number of people that actually came to that gig. For example if your band made £500 from shirts one night, that may sound like a reasonable return. But if the band actually played to 1000 people then the maths works out at 50 pence per head! Not quite so impressive, is it. If you then project this scenario onto a company like Bravado they would use this equation to estimate exactly how much of an advance they would give you for your next tour, and it wouldn't be much.

Merchandising companies, like all companies involved in business, look at the facts, i.e. what gigs are the band playing, how many people should they be playing to, and do they actually think that the tour will sell out. It is not unusual for Bravado to work out their initial figures on the presumption that there will only be a 70 per cent attendance during the tour. 'It is hard' Maria explains:

> 'it's a real gamble, and if people are looking for an advance from us, they may say 'well we want £100,000' and they have not even looked at the number of people that they are going to be playing to. It's just a figure that they want but we've then got to make it work, and if it doesn't we've then got to go back and try to explain to them why we've done that. It's not that we don't want to give them the money because they're not worth it, ultimately everybody has to make money out of it, and it is hard work. We've given money to bands in the past and they have sunk without a trace! And bands always disappear when they owe you money. Promoters will say that they are the ones taking the gamble and that merchandisers are just like a monkey, you get on their backs and ride with them. But it is a gamble for everyone, we are talking huge money now, because a few years ago £25,000 was a huge sum to give to a band. Now some bands won't even pick up the phone unless you're talking £150,000. It's so ridiculous that some of them we basically laugh out of the room.'

Ultimately a T-shirt can be many things; For the fan it can be a fashion statement, it tells others about a band and it tells others that you like that band. For the band itself, at one level it can mean being able to afford the petrol to get home from a gig or just another cardboard box full of stuff in your garage. At another level it can mean huge advances, a great income and masses of long-term advertising that someone else has paid for. Not bad for a cheap undergarment, is it?

On the road

t is all too easy to talk about a band of any level of popularity playing gigs, be it on a local basis or a world tour. However, many bands actually struggle to get started, even in their local pub. This chapter looks at where to play, how to go about getting into the venues, and how to make the best of a gig situation by being prepared. It is easy to fall into the trap of believing that a gig is just a rehearsal in front of people. Gigs are nerve-racking, they can induce vomiting, they are capable of producing pure exhilaration and total annihilation. Do not presume that your band will automatically be well received. Be warned ...

Hustling for work

Now the band has hopefully written a full set's worth of songs (a 'set' can be anything from a 15 minute showcase to an hour and a half depending on where the gig is). As a rule of thumb it is a good idea to accept that an average set length for pubs, clubs and support slots is between 35 and 45 minutes, which is between eight and ten songs. These tracks should be rehearsed to a point where they feel ready to be performed live! There are two immediate reasons for wanting to play live: one is to start to build a fan base, the second is to learn the craft of playing live.

It is imperative here to remember that, when it comes to performing, if something can go wrong it probably will. In the immortal words of the scouts; Be prepared! A lot of bands tend to underestimate just how many gigs they need to do to compete with world class acts.

An added complication is the fact that there are less gigs and music venues available for bands to cut their teeth on. Regardless of this a band should be aiming to play around three or four times a week, on a regular basis, if they are going to be able to compete with the professional bands. The gigs are thin on the ground, but they still exist and the bands that mean business will be out there doing the business.

The first show

Most bands under the age of eighteen will begin their gigging lives either playing at their local youth club or school hall, and inviting their mates down. If either of these venues are not keen to rent out the venue for a gig, it may be a good idea to promote and hold the gig in aid of a local charity and charge a pound or so to get in. For the first timers a good tip is to never underestimate the length of time it will take to prepare for a gig. The chances are that you will have to arrange a small vocal PA, maybe some stage blocks, and even a few lights and a smoke machine. All these things must be arranged in advance as you will look extremely foolish trying to get it sorted out on the morning of the gig, and slowly realising that you cannot. You will also need to publicise the gig, as playing your first gig to nobody can be soul destroying.

Do your best to ensure that your are paying for as little of this stuff as possible because otherwise it will all add up to an amount that may well be hard to recoup on the door. Get the posters done in an art class at school and ask to use the school photocopier to duplicate them. See if any older local bands will lend you their vocal PA. Check the school theatre for lights, etc.

Playing-wise, band members must be as prepared as possible, because it is quite a shock playing in front of an audience for the first time. Any musician will tell the story of how terrifying their first gig was, and many very successful musicians still throw up before a gig because they are so nervous.

Also remember that musical equipment has a habit of going wrong. If one of your guitar leads works reasonably well most of the time, it will definitely go wrong during the first song of the set. Not only will this put you and the rest of the band off from the start, it will also undermine your confidence for the rest of the gig ultimately leading to a disastrous show. Always ensure that, within reason, you have as much new stuff as possible or try to carry spares. Even if you have brand new effects pedals with brand new patch leads joining them together, and you are feeling confident, it is guaranteed that the singer will leap on them from a great height during a song and destroy one of the leads. It will then take you a good minute or two to find out which one is knackered, by which time the song is over and you have not played an audible note for the last half of it.

A golden rule for the early gigs is to keep your set up, and your playing, as simple as possible. There is enough to worry about when standing on stage in front of a hundred of your mates who are all waiting for you to trip up. So by narrowing the odds of this happening, you will have a good gig, and your mates in the audience will be pleasantly surprised. But with all the preparation in the world things still go wrong, as Bruce remembers:

> 'I remember getting a machine head stuck up our singer's nose. I must have swung the guitar round quickly and he happened to be in the wrong place at the wrong time. When we pulled it out there was a lot of blood – but the show went on. Leads and ped-alboards were always a problem and we decided early on that it was definitely worth paying for quality products. I always preferred a hard wire rather than a radio for reliability and sound. The other problem we had to sort out quickly in the early days was tuning. You need a guitar with solid intonation that doesn't go out too quickly under lights. It's also a good idea to learn how to put strings on properly. A good guitar tech can change a set of guitar strings in five minutes and have them stretched in tuned up and ready to go.'

Check the set

If we are performing musicians we are primarily entertainers. A show should be entertaining and distinctly different to stringing a few songs together. Every aspect of the performance is important and great artists are instinctively aware of the attention to detail needed to hold an audience's attention.

The 'classic' set starts with some form of 'impact song', something that is exciting and is definitive of the band's sound (often a crowd favourite or a hit record for the act). The next two or three songs should be at least as powerful as the first and segued together keeping and building the excitement level. At this point the set can drop down in pace into either less adrenalised tracks or slower, ballad-style songs. The singer can take the time to communicate with the audience at this point. During the middle of the set changes of clothes, set and instrumentation help to keep the attention of the audience. The set can then gradually increase in intensity finishing on a high, usually with the band's most popular track saved for the encore.

Strangely getting the order of the songs right is far more crucial than how well you play for the audience. Get the beginning and end

TIP

An audience can be built up to a frenzy even before the show starts. Dimming the house lights creates a powerful feeling of expectancy. The longer the audience can be kept waiting the more the excitement builds.

of the set happening and you are 50 per cent of the way there. Most punters remember the excitement of the beginning and end of a show more than the details in the middle. Great bands exploit this by drawing out the intros to a set with intro tapes, lighting and sound effects.

What comes next?

Whilst spontaneity in performance can be magical, do not introduce it into your live work until you are completely in control of the situation. Once you have decided on your set list, rehearse it as a set. Use rehearsals to play the set straight through a number of times, and time it to make sure it is not too long or too short. Spend time memorising which song comes next if you can, as this will leave you free to concentrate not only on the song you are playing, but you will also be ready for any setting changes that are needed in between songs. Whilst it is important to have one, try not to rely on a set list as these are as likely to be destroyed by your singer or audience as your patch leads are. It is a great idea to record rehearsals, as this will not only highlight the musical areas needing work, it will also show you how long the gaps between the songs are. It is a good idea to practise the links between songs, rehearse the intros and outros and guitar and clothing changes, especially if you have not done many gigs. Remember the singer has the responsibility of introducing songs and of generally being the voice of the band, so if he or she has not worked out anything to say the gaps between songs can become vast and can make the band look amateurish. Try and work out some set patter for the singer to practise, because you will never know when you will have to tune up or put your bass drum pedal back on your bass drum. Ultimately the best advice is to plan everything, every single word that is going to be sung, every single lick that will be played on the guitar, every single drum fill, every single link between songs. Strangely enough this will allow you to have a more spontaneous gig.

TIP

*K*nowing that there is a well-rehearsed plan of action to fall back on gives the performer the confidence to go out on a limb and try something 'off the cuff.'

Let's go down the pub

The pub is one of the main venues for up and coming bands, and this is where young bands will get most of their initial experience of playing in front of an audience which is not totally made up of their friends and family. Getting a gig in a local boozer that regularly promotes live music is not difficult. Even so, too many bands delegate one member to phone up the landlord or manager, and if the phone is engaged they give up and fall at the first fence. If the phone is engaged, then try again! Eventually you will get through and the chances are that the manager will say that he or she has never heard of you and will not be prepared to chance booking an unknown local band. Do not give up at this hurdle either, go to the pub and meet the manager, give them a demo tape and a biography and tell them that you are capable of filling his pub with punters. Pubs will give gigs to bands who are organised enough to have a demo pack, but they are even more likely to give you a gig if you promise them a full house. Remember however that if you do play that venue and no one turns up, it will be the first and last time you ever play there!

Do not rely on just one place, spend an evening or two visiting every pub in the local area and try to put together a little tour of the area. It may be a good idea to join forces with another local band for these gigs, which will not only give a full night's live music, it will also double the number of people in the pub and ensure that the manager is happy with the attendance. It is worth noting that even if the venue does not have a license for live music they are still legally entitled to allow a duo to play. Many bands have an acoustic set which can be performed in this way.

There are two types of pubs that can be considered, there is the local pub that might put on live music once a fortnight, and there is the live music pub that will put on bands two or three times a week. On a local level these live music pubs will usually have a stage, a few lights and a small PA, but when you reach the big cities these pubs are far more professional and are considered reputable venues in their own right – most will have live music every night of the week.

A good example of this type of pub venue is the King's Head in Fulham, London. Although essentially a pub, the King's Head has a great history of live music and many big names have graced its stage. The live room has a good-sized stage, good lights, on stage monitors and a great PA. It also has in-house video facilities so that the bands can film their performance to use either as a promotional tool or to see where they are going wrong. It has also recently opened an acoustic room upstairs for more intimate performances.

This style of venue is another step up the ladder and as a result will be harder to get into; bands that play these venues have often played many times in pubs and other small local venues and are now looking to heighten their profile up to a semi-professional level. A band should be pulling at least a hundred people to make it worthwhile and to make the promoter want to book the band again (if your band is not based in London, then this is where coaches come in handy). It is also worth remembering that while you will be lucky to get free beer for a night at your local pub, at somewhere like the Kings Head you will receive a pound for every flyer that is handed in at the door by one of the band's supporters. Regardless of this step up in the venue stakes it is still relatively easy to get the gig if you are professional about your approach and you are happy to play on a Monday night at 8.00pm initially.

Don't get lost

Performance-wise however the situation is very different. Firstly

It's easy to get carried away
in the soundcheck

you must be able to cope with playing through a large PA system,
maybe using pieces of equipment that you are not familiar with.
Also there will be at least two other bands on that night, you must
be able to handle monitors on the stage. It is also possible that the
in-house sound engineer will not be very experienced (but believes
he is the best in the world). Luckily this is not true at the King's
Head!

One of the main problems that most bands have when hitting a
semi-professional stage for the first time is that they sound terrible
through a PA. This all comes down to preparation, it is perfectly
possible to be playing at a venue with three or four other bands and
to be on stage, set up and ready to go in 15 minutes, and sound
great. However if there are fundamental problems with the act's
playing styles or arrangement skills, even the best PA and
soundman won't be able to save the gig.

Tips for playing live

One of the main mistakes that any guitarist (bass, lead or rhythm)
or keyboard player can make is standing above their amp. This
results in it being impossible to hear the real sound that is coming
out of the amp because it is being projected under the performer's
legs straight into the audience. As a direct result, the amp will be
too loud for the sound engineer to control and will almost certainly
be too trebly. If, as a guitarist, you go and stand out in the
audience, about 20 feet away from the stage, you may be shocked
at how awful your sound is. So watch out for the volume, remember
that the more control that you can give the sound engineer to
control the better. After all what is the point of playing through a

large PA, if you are so loud that you cannot be put in the mix? If one member of the band is too loud then the others may turn themselves up to be heard. This then leads to the sound engineer turning up the lead vocal in an effort to balance the mix. The result? A lead vocal that will certainly feedback and an overall band sound that is completely out of control.

Your first point of reference for volume will be the drums. An acoustic kit needs to be played at a certain volume to sound like a drum kit, and it will be loud in a rock situation. If you have a good drummer with 'ears' then the kit will sound balanced and musical. He or she will play sympathetically with the vocal, perhaps closing hi hats during a verse and leaving room in the arrangement to ensure the music and the song come across.

Bad drummers with little technique will not be able to tune their kits properly, and will not understand the basics of tone production. Here are some areas to work on in your own arrangements. If you listen to professional recordings and analyse the arrangements and construction you will learn many practical lessons which you can apply to your own work with instant results.

Drums

If the bass drum work is too busy or inconsistent, it will be difficult to lock onto a groove. If you listen to most of the records in the top forty, it is striking how simple and repetitive most of the grooves are. If there is a fill it is carefully constructed to set up the next section or to fulfil a specific need in the track. Consistency is the key to drawing people into a record from a groove perspective. A common problem with many bands is that the drummer makes up the bass drum pattern as he goes along. The licks may be hard to do and satisfying from a technical point of view but very distracting to the listener.

Music first started in primitive times with repetitive rhythms (probably two sticks being banged together). We are still instinctively drawn to rhythmic repetition and any clubber will affirm the power of a repetitive four to the floor bass drum to induce trance like states. The opposite effect is produced when the bass drum is over complex and constantly changing. The listener is 'locked out of the track' and their interest wanes. Again it is imperative to be accurate with the snare drum, both in tone and timing. Good drummers know where their snare drum sounds best and practice hitting it in the same spot every time, producing a consistent and musical sound that can drive the band. The top end of the kit (cymbals and hats) can sonically either be rounded and musical in the hands of a good player or harsh, thin and unpleasant if technique is bad. Some lessons from a professional may be needed to help a drummer achieve a professional sound.

Bass guitar

Bass frequencies can be a nightmare in a gig situation and a rumbling, out of control, bass guitar, mars many a performance. Again bad playing technique is the chief culprit. Particular attention should be paid to the left hand fretting technique and the right hand. Good players are capable of producing a tight punchy tone that is audible in the mix at low volume. This negates the desire of the player to keep turning up the volume in an effort to hear themselves and allows a natural mix at reasonable level.

Electric guitar and keyboards

The electric guitar can be a hideous instrument in the wrong hands! Good guitarists always leave space for the vocalist in their playing, watch their level and are usually very concerned with the frequencies that they choose. The guitar needs to sit comfortably in the sonic space between the top end of the kit and the bass guitar. Bad guitarists usually have little or no middle frequencies in their guitar sound, just top end that will compete with the cymbals and loads of bottom end competing with the bass. They end up with a 'fizzy' sound that cannot be heard very well. Lacking any definition they then turn up, in an effort to hear themselves more clearly, not understanding that volume does not equal definition. The top kit will still compete with the guitar and the drummer will probably be playing louder in an effort to hear himself above the guitar. The audience will be suffering and probably leaving. Great guitar tones are often boxy and middley on their own but these tones will sit much better in the overall sonic space. Similarly a keyboard player should choose his or her frequencies from the spaces in the arrangement. A keyboard player in a hard rock outfit, competing with two loud distorted guitars, will have much less sonic freedom than a player in a dance project with the whole sonic spectrum to experiment with.

Don't be a speed king

One of the great things about playing live is the huge rush of adrenaline that musicians experience when they step out onto the stage. If the whole band becomes really excited and nervous about playing in front of an audience, this can have a direct result upon the tempo of the songs, usually driving them way above what they actually sound best at. The importance of getting the tempos of the songs right in a live situation cannot be overstated, and to this end it is an extremely good idea to rehearse to a click. Ideally this would be produced by a small drum machine, like a Dr Rhythm, linked to a pair of headphones that the drummer could then wear. But if this is out of the band's budget, then just having a metronome set to the

TIP

Recording all gigs and listening back to them will give you the best possible insight into how your band played. It is not necessarily important that the songs were played perfectly note for note, after all it is a gig and the band should have been trying to put on a show as well as play. What is important is that the tempos are right, the gaps between songs are not too long, and that the band performed well as a unit.

correct speed before starting each song is preferable to nothing at all. If a track feels good at 120 beats per minute in rehearsal, then it should not be played at 140 bpm in a gig situation. An out of control band will make an audience feel 'uncomfortable'.

Ultimately there is no mystery to being a good live band; the basics are there for all if care is taken to ensure that they are put in place. Good live bands are entertaining, tight, in tune, in time, the set is well ordered and the song tempos are right.

Earning money on the road

Before we leap into the back of a Transit van we need to be clear on why we are gigging in the first place. This is particularly important when an act is releasing product. Once your band is into the serious business of making records then you need to make sure that the timing of the tours are carefully planned around the release of the records for maximum benefit in terms of sales and chart placement. Touring will also create press opportunities in the form of interviews and reviews which again will be most effective if they are timed alongside a single or album campaign. You can also make considerable revenue on the road if you plan your budgets carefully – but beware because you can also lose money very easily if you get it wrong.

The last reason for touring is to have fun and to play your own music to an appreciative audience. This is after all the reason why you started playing in the first place. When we were younger most of us didn't imagine ourselves sitting in a lawyer's office or setting up a limited company when we stood in front of the mirror playing air guitar! We pictured ourselves on a big stage under lights with a

'I don't care what it's been, what is it now'. Life on the road means eating whenever you can

crowd of thousands of screaming fans just like our heroes in our record collection.

Unfortunately, until you get to the big league, the reality of touring will be less glamorous than you might expect. Imagine a band who have released their first single on an indie label and have booked a three week tour round the UK. The band is relatively unknown and can only attract gig fees of £100 a night. The venues are small clubs and well-known venues on the circuit like Leeds Duchess of York, Bath Moles Club, London's Bull and Gate etc. There is no money for hotels and unless the band can crash at some willing fan, groupie, or relation's house they will have to sleep in the van on top of the backline. This is the tour from hell and all the authors of this book have been there. Here's a typical daily budget:

Touring budget

Van Hire	£40
Petrol	£25
Food for five	£25
Sundries (strings, maps, fuses, picks etc)	£10

As you can see £100 doesn't leave much room for manoeuvre. There are hundreds of bands on this circuit and the ability to survive it can be a big part in the act's ultimate success. It's very difficult to eat for £5 a day and even if the venue provides a hot meal it's often barely edible. Ill health is a problem and lack of sleep can cause the mildest mannered band members to become argumentative. If the band can survive and come out the other side of two or three of these transit van tours they usually find they have become musically and personally tighter. The pace of life is fast when a band is in a different town every day and this constant flow of new experiences is very healthy for the song writers in the project who often produce some of their best work at this stage.

Another imaginary three-week tour may have a completely different budget. This time the band has had a few top forty hits and is playing large theatre type venues and small sports halls with capacities around two to three thousand. In this instance the promoter has taken all the financial risk and guaranteed the band £100,000 gig fees with a split on the door money once the attendance averages over 80 per cent on the tour (this is called 'breaking PC.'). The band must then budget for all their expenses out of gig fees. These expenses will include:

PA and lights

It is usual to do a deal with a PA company which will include the rig, monitors, staff (out front sound, monitor engineer, humpers and drivers). The deal may also include specialist backline techs and a stage manager. Sometimes the lighting will be included in the deal and sometimes a separate company will provide it. It is possible to spend the entire budget and much more just on lights alone so the band or their tour manager must work out a sensible compromise between quality and cost.

The authors would suggest that an independent tour manager with no conflict of interest would be better placed to advise the band. The deal should be inclusive of trucking and transport for roadies and equipment, which will usually travel independently of the band.

Hotels

The band will probably want to stay in hotels every night. Very good hotels can be booked in advance through a travel agent at reasonable rates and if the whole tour is booked as a single booking it is often just as cheap to stay in quality hotels as dodgy guest houses. Hotels are usually very accommodating to bands and sympathetic to their requirements, which range from late checkouts to keeping the bar open all night.

The tour budget does not usually cover individual band members bar bills, phone bills or cheeseburgers on room service at two in the morning.

Playing gigs can be tiring

Band transport

The band can travel in a variety of different ways. It is possible to hire a purpose built tour bus with bunks, video and even a bar. When the novelty wears off these buses are actually quite uncomfortable and for travelling the modest distances around the UK many bands prefer a fast large estate or 'space wagon' type vehicle. These can be hired from any major car hire centre and are reliable, fast and comfortable.

Equipment

There should be room in the budget for breakages and wear and tear of the band's backline and guitars etc. The constant load-in and outs are very hard on the gear and it is amazing how quickly delicate items such as keyboards and valve amps can wear out on the road. Strings, which would last three weeks in rehearsal, may need to be changed every day and pedals and radio mikes will eat batteries. The whole stage is usually held together by a wonderful substance – gaffer tape. Very sticky and very strong, it's also expensive and you'll need a lot of it on a three-week tour.

Catering

A band may decide to hire a catering company to provide food for the band and crew. The caterers will travel to the venue and set up a kitchen and restaurant in the backstage area of the gig. The food is usually very good. Some band members can start to look quite podgy half way into the tour.

Where the hell is everybody?

Insurance

The PA and lighting companies will look after their own third party insurance but the band will need to be covered in case a fan is injured by a flying plectrum or whatever and tries to sue. It is more or less impossible to get cover for a band who wishes to protect itself against not being able to do a gig through illness.

When on the road ill health is a fact of life and insurance companies know how often singers will experience voice problems when touring. There are many tales of singers with terrible croaky voices being given a shot of cortisone up the rear from the doc and being pushed out onto the stage because the band couldn't afford to cancel the gig.

It's easy to see how this lifestyle can become addictive, a new city every day and no worries or responsibilities. But for some successful artists when the weeks become months and the months become years living life out of a suitcase can become very hard work indeed.

A typical day on the road

This is a typical day's events for a band touring the city halls of the UK.

9am	band and tour manager meet in the lobby of the hotel. One member of the band is usually still in bed and some musicians are nursing hangovers. Everybody is in a bad mood. Some members are staring in disbelief at their bar, phone and pay-to-view low quality pornography bill.
9.20am	the guilty party is finally roused from his pit and has hurriedly packed, leaving half his clothes in the hotel.
9.30am	band hits the road with a long drive ahead of them.
10.30am	stop at Little Chef for breakfast. Nobody has eaten in the hotel despite it being included in the deal because it is served too early. Little Chef Big Breakfasts save the day and band morale is improving.
4pm	band arrives at venue. The road crew have travelled earlier and have set up the PA and backline and are now soundchecking the bass drum at gig level
5pm	the bass drum soundcheck has just finished there is a brief linecheck of the other instruments and the band shuffle onstage play half a song. There is usually an argument about monitor levels at this point.
5.30pm	back to the hotel for a sleep
7.30	back to the venue. There are hundreds of people queuing outside the gig and the band start to get excited and lively for the first time in the day.
8pm	nervous members of the band will be pacing, peeing and being sick prior to going onstage. Many acts have strange rituals, which they believe will bring them good luck during the gig. These range from silly songs and chants to dark unmentionable practices too dark and unmentionable to mention.
8.30 – 9.30pm	band onstage having a great time. They come offstage buzzing with adrenaline.
9.30pm	band get stuck into rider (a rider is an extra paragraph on a promoter's contract and usually refers to the drinks and refreshments in the

	band's dressing room). A typical rider for a rock 'n' roll band would be two bottles of spirits, four bottles of wine and a crate of fizzy lager.
9.35pm	band are pissed as rats
10.30pm	band disperse to various night clubs, parties and dives. More civilised musicians head back to the hotel bar for a quiet drink.
11pm	a discreet veil is drawn over the debauched proceedings at this point.
6am	the last band member falls asleep.
9am	the cycle repeats itself

Tribute bands

Struggling along trying to come up with the next 'big thing' is not the only way to gain access to the performing world of music. Many musicians join or form bands in the first place because they have been influenced and inspired by other bands or musicians to either sing or play an instrument. A great way to not only play music that you love and earn money while you are doing it is to form a tribute band, which you could either concentrate on solely as a main form of income or get involved with alongside your original band.

Paying tribute to your influences in this way will not only help to pay the bills, it will also develop discipline in your playing ability and teach you new styles, giving you access to knowledge that the 'I refuse to prostitute my art' musicians will never have or understand fully. If the thought of playing in a tribute band is not top of your priority list because you do not believe that it can go anywhere, just remember the success that Bjorn Again have had. They went from an Abba covers band to world-wide recognised stars who play all the big festivals to thousands of people every year, and they are not alone. If you think about it for a minute the chances are that you have seen tribute bands performing at festivals near you.

Pretending to be the
Pretenders

Paying tribute

Once you have decided on the band or style of music that you wish
to cover, it is time to find out about tribute band management.
There are many companies that specialise in this form of
entertainment such as Psycho Management, who are based in
London and Godalming near Guildford, and Entertainment UK who
are also based in London. This is what Patrick Haveron from Psycho
Management had to say about their role:

> 'Really we are an agency more than a management company
> because most of our musicians have a certain level of compe-
> tence in management. It is not like an original scene where it is
> much harder to get a break, a manager has to know the record
> companies and the publishing companies and what kind of deals
> that they have to do. As far as deals are concerned in this field it
> really is 'what are you going to get paid for your live appear-
> ance?', what is your fee? It's all down to that, really. So we are
> agents for anything and everything and for that we generally
> charge 15 per cent which is the industry standard for agents. We
> do do some management which is really wiping bottoms for peo-
> ple, but we try to get out of that because it is a time consuming
> thing. This is really a live business and it's not that complicated,
> most people know what they are going to do. They have to be
> somewhere at 4.00pm for soundcheck, they are on stage at
> 10.00pm, they'll pick up a cheque for x amount and then they'll
> go home.'

Gig packs and packed gigs

The most important functions of a tribute management company are, firstly, getting a band's publicity right, because it is all down to the marketing of a band as to whether they will get booked. This is not so important for an established act because people know what Bjorn Again or the Bootleg Beatles do, but less well known acts will need to concentrate on promotional tools like videos, tapes, photographs and biographies that are presented in a professional way. A tribute management company will not be able to sell a new or little heard of band without these things.

The second important factor is actually getting the gigs because a management company could sign up a band who may be great, but if they cannot get that band any gigs they will have to be honest from the start. Too many agencies promise the earth and then do not deliver. A tribute management company should have their fingers on the fashion pulse, knowing what it is that the public want to see, and understanding why a specific act will be well received.

Spiced or Strangled?

Recently Psycho Management advertised for a Spice Girls outfit to work with. Once that was up and running some of the Spice Girls split off to form an All Saints tribute act, and now one of the girls has got involved in an Aqua tribute band. This demonstrates the difference between those who understand the financial aspect of the fashionable tribute scene as opposed to a band like The Men In Black, a Stranglers tribute act who formed the group because the members all have a love of the band and want to play their music. Those who move from one fashionable pop band to another in order to keep up with the ever shifting tide of pop music and fashion, are far more financially motivated and understand the marketability of such tribute acts. These people understand that they will get a good amount of paying gigs for at least six months before moving on. One the other hand The Men In Black are not going to make that sort of money, however they will be able to find a reasonably successful market for the band, which would probably include festivals in countries like Germany where the Stranglers are still revered. They would not however be able to play on such a regular basis as the fashion conscious pop tribute acts.

These are the two aspects of tribute bands, but if a band is signed on with an agency like Psycho it ultimately comes down to one thing: cash. For example if there are two agencies fighting for a gig and one drops his commission to a lesser amount, then the band will simply go with that agent. Also if two bands are being considered for a gig but the venue or organisers of the event are

An old routine for The New
Recruits

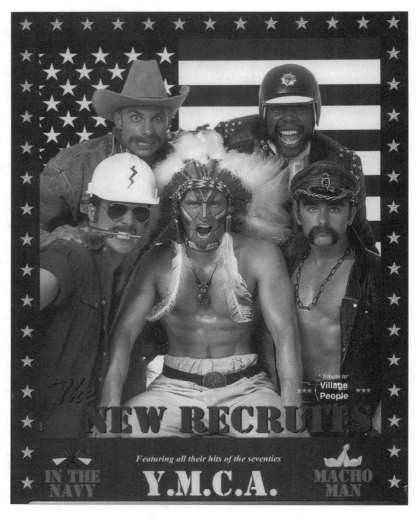

concerned about the amount of money they have to spend, they will
just give the gig to the band most open to negotiation.

There are a few simple rules to follow if the thought of a tribute
band appeals; firstly, decide what sort of band you are going to be,
then contact that band's fan club to see how many other tribute
bands are doing it. Secondly, it is always a good idea to choose a
band that is no longer together, as you should be able to appeal to
that band's fan base. Lastly, be convincing in your appearance and
in your playing, no fan wants to see a tribute band who believe they
can better the originals.

What bands?

It is unlikely that a tribute management company will specialise in one style of music or entertainment. Most are not averse to a broad register of acts, as long as that act has some sort of angle, because they are constantly looking to fill the specific requirements of their customers. There are many examples of initially curious acts that one would not think could possibly make a living out of their chosen art, who actually do very well. Psycho have an act on the books at the moment called the Ukelele Kings who consist of drums, bass, and lead and rhythm ukelele. The band pride themselves on their versions of The Prodigy's Firestarter and Nirvana's Smells Like Teen Spirit, but they cover all modern styles including Oasis and the Spice Girls. Another curious hit is Mr Methane who dresses in a green batman-style outfit, lies on a table and farts along to tunes such as How Much Is That Doggy In The Window.

From the rather amusing end of the scale, it can then turn nasty with acts such as The Carnival Of Freaks, which includes The Chaos Clowns who impale themselves on sharp objects and a woman who hangs weights from her vagina. While all this sounds a million miles away from your band these are not the only acts by any means, just think of a band you like and it is guaranteed that there is a tribute band out there covering their music and image. There are limitations to this though, as Patrick Haveron described:

> 'Anything that will sell, we'll take on. But we are honest with bands and say OK that's our fifth Pink Floyd tribute, we don't get many Pink Floyd gigs as it is. Or say you're a Meat Loaf tribute and you're based in Scotland ...well we don't think we're going to be able to get you much work, to be honest. Or even Frank Zappa, we've got two Zappa tributes and muso's love Frank Zappa, it's that learning the licks thing. But I just can't get them arrested because only other muso's will go and see it really, and it's probably only worth £200 to £400 if you can get it up to that level. I got a fax through from a friend who runs the Cavern Club in Liverpool, and he's got 82 Beatles bands on his books. Bands have to have some responsibility for selling themselves and being saleable.'

Where the...?

The markets for this style of band are quite diverse and they need to be if a management company is to keep a stock of 130 tribute bands, 30-40 cover bands and various curiosities in work. An act of any sort can expect to play at corporate functions and Christmas parties, weddings, student unions, live music venues, pubs and

Killer Queen – arguably the best of a host of Queen tribute bands

INFO

Remember that PRS (Performing Right Society) payments are not down to the band, they are down to the venue who should present the band with a form to fill in listing all the songs they have performed that night. Also there is no copyright infringement because it is a live show, as long as you are not attempting to pass yourself off as the real band.

festivals. For live music venues in particular, the acts that will be most successful are those that are faithful to the original bands that they are covering, have attention to detail and more than likely come from the rock/blues sphere. Good examples are bands who cover The Doors, Nirvana, The Who, The Police, Jimi Hendrix, Oasis, etc.

The most successful acts cover bands that were, or are, stadium bands because these bands obviously were and are very successful in their own right. Many venues are now relying on tribute bands to fill their dance floors, purely because they know that people will come and see them because they have heard of them before. Remember that, especially in major cities, the public have grown weary of going down to their local pub or club to see a band that they have not heard of, because there are so many bands out there that are not very good. Medium sized venues like the Mean Fiddler in Harlesden, the Standard in Walthamstow and the Venue in New Cross now rely on the pull of a good tribute band because of the novelty factor as well as the fan factor.

The most important point to make is that if you are going to do tribute, you must do it well. If you do it well then there are hundreds of gigs to do and lots of money to be made. All this and you get to play music that you love.

So you win again

For those who think that a tribute band will get no further than the corporate Christmas party, it might be a good time to consider the success of Bjorn Again. If there was a 'glass ceiling' in the field of tribute bands, then they have successfully managed to smash straight through it into the main stream pop world. They have had hits in the charts by covering Erasure songs in an Abba style, and this was reciprocated by Erasure who replied with an Abba song done in the high energy Erasure style. While this demonstrates a superb piece of marketing strategy, their success is also because Abba have been incredibly popular for many years, and still are, while the original band no longer exists. So Bjorn Again not only get very well paid for their shows, they have also gained access to the big stage because of the success of the original band plus the humour of the tribute band.

An example of Bjorn Again's almost unique position in the music world was displayed when Nirvana played the Reading Rock festival, and insisted in their contract that they were to be supported by Bjorn Again. Now they do festivals all over Europe, America and Australia, where the tribute scene originated, and they are almost seen as an original band simply because you cannot see Abba any more.

For many, success may never be as big as Bjorn Again, but this does not mean that tribute artists cannot make a healthy living out of their chosen star or stars. Whatever people may think of the television program 'Stars In Their Eyes', the contestants that do the show are examples of how good you can be at tribute, and therefore how much money you can earn. Do these performers go on to make a living in tribute after the show? When asked this question Patrick Haveron from Psycho Management replied:

'Yes, if they want to they can. One of the success stories we've been involved with is Rob Lamberti who was a roofer from Scunthorpe. He won his show as George Michael, and came second in the whole series that year to the Marti Pellow guy. He's given up his £300 a week job and he probably now earns a £1000 a week easily just from touring round doing personal appearances, doing night clubs, doing stuff with a band. The Prince guy, Mark Anthony, from Stars In Their Eyes was a plumber from Catford but now he gets five or six hundred pounds for a show because he is such a double, it's really scary. He's presented Top Of The Pops, he doubles for him in places like Switzerland where he is treated like royalty.'

Who comes first?

What has to be remembered at this point is that these tribute agencies are not working solely for the tribute band, they are also supplying a service to their customers and as such have to strike a careful balance between the two sides. On the one hand it is imperative to sell the customer what they want.

If a management company only represents a couple of bands then you must get them work all the time. On the other hand the companies like Psycho Management and Entertainment UK operate on a much larger scale, so if the customer wants a seventies disco band then the tribute company chooses whichever act fits the budget from their list of disco bands, and that's the one they get. However if the tribute company are specifically managing a seventies disco act like Disco Inferno, it is their duty to get them work by pushing them into the most suitable position if possible.

Of course it is not the end of the world if the company settles on another band as the agency will still receive their 15 per cent. It can be a question of balance, but this is made easier for those agencies who retain a large number of bands on their lists.

There are two things that bands should do to ensure regular work; Firstly, be readily available and easily contactable. This means having an organised and regularly updated diary, and giving the agency access to that diary so they can see at a glance when a band is free. It also means having a mobile phone, as one of the biggest complaints from agencies concerns the difficulty in contacting acts immediately to suggest or confirm bookings. Secondly, strike up a rapport with the agency. Remember companies like Psycho or Entertainment UK have a long list of acts and they cannot have them all at the forefront of their thoughts.

A good idea is to phone them on a reasonably regular basis, say once every fortnight, just to remind them that you are still alive and eager for work. It is a good idea to try to speak to the same member of staff every time and build a relationship with them. Don't hassle them or be a pain because this will lose you gigs, just stay in contact and be friendly.

Ultimately the band comes first because the agency's contract will be weighted towards them in terms of riders, facilities and actually getting paid on the night of the gig. Many corporate customers want to pay within thirty days, but this style of entertainment is very much an immediate business and bands should expect to be paid on the night of the performance.

Agencies will do their best to maintain a good working relationship with a large percentage of their acts, but if they fall out with a band then they will not or cannot book that band again. However many tribute bands still maintain the ethos of the original rock bands.

There have been many instances where a tribute band has trashed a dressing room or stolen stuff from the venue, or been late for a gig or forgotten a passport, all of which can cause problems. Unfortunately many bands tend to believe that they are indispensable, which of course is not true in many cases. Patrick Haveron explained some examples of what can happen:

'We had a client in Finland who had seen a chap who does Bryan Adams in our brochure. Well he was pretty disorganised and didn't have a passport even though he was thirty years old, so he had to get his birth certificate from his mum. Well his mum hadn't told him that his dad wasn't his real father, so he wasn't actually who he thought he was. She had to sit him down and tell him this, complete crisis! Then he had to get a solicitors letter backing this up because now his drivers licence was no good, his bank details were no good, because he wasn't who he thought he was. In the end he didn't get the gig because he couldn't get his passport.

There was a situation with the Spiced Girls where some of the girls left and formed Spice It Up. Then Spice It Up turned up at a Spiced Girls gig and tried to get some of their costumes back, and a cat fight developed between the two groups and we had to get them out the side door to their dressing room! That story made the Guardian and then got syndicated around America and appeared in the New York Times.

There's one guy in the Kamikaze Freak Show who regularly puts his head in a bucket of fire crackers and then lets them off. One day he forgot to put his ear plugs in and blew his ear drum out. Another guy from the show fires fireworks as a finale from his bottom, and one of those back fired and he had a very burnt ring in Camden Hospital.

The Brit Girls

On a more basic side of things if a band decide they want 48 bottles of lager, two bottles of wine and a bottle of champagne, well some organisers just get upset about that saying "we don't want the band being drunk at our event, so we'll just cancel it and get somebody else".'

Ultimately tribute is about performing for money, but there is much to gain from this style of band other than cash. If you are good at tribute then you will not only be building your arsenal of songs and extending your playing or singing technique, you will also get to play at venues that an original band may never get the opportunity to play. You will also bypass the difficulty of getting people to come and support your music because it is not something new, it is something that they will be familiar with and probably love. Many musicians understand the problems of breaking new and original music onto an unsuspecting audience.

If you are no good at tribute then at least you have tried. You will still have learned some songs that you probably could not play before and you will have gone out and played in the local pub, thus getting some extra live experience which will be invaluable in your future as an original artist.

Legal eagles **10**

If you are going to make it in the music business, the chances are at some point you are going to need a lawyer. Everybody wants to sign a recording deal, but do you know what it is you are signing? The vast majority of artists who sign a record deal also sign a publishing deal, but do you know why or what it is? In these two questions lies the basic and yet essential reasoning behind getting a good lawyer. When it comes to signing a contract an experienced manager (not your mate who's got a car and a suit) will know what they want because they will have had experience of doing deals. However a manager may only do a couple of deals a year while a specialist music lawyer will be sorting out contracts on an almost daily basis. And before you say something like 'but I can't afford a lawyer', remember that music history is littered with stories of bands who have been ripped off by their label, by their publisher, by their manager, etc ...

Who's the guy in the suit?

Andrew Myers, now one of the most experienced music lawyers around, originally trained as a lawyer with a firm call Clifford Chance having studied at Leeds University and law school in London. Being a music lover he wanted to get into music law, so he applied to various record companies and law firms, but Clintons of Covent Garden, London was at the top of his list and they offered him a job.

Andrew Myers

Clintons is one of the longest established entertainment law firms, having been around since the sixties, and has acted for clients as diverse as Jimi Hendrix, Paul McCartney, Michael Jackson, and is still at the cutting edge of music acting for U2, Paul Weller, Stereophonics, Daft Punk and Peter Andre to name but a few.

Andrew's role in the firm is music, including acting on behalf of new bands and taking them from unknown acts, through the period of breaking and on from there. One of the most intriguing points about Andrew from a new band's perspective is that, whilst lawyers are notoriously expensive and therefore sometimes deemed unfeasible, he is able to be extremely flexible over fees. His viewpoint is somewhat like that of a record company in that he is looking for long termism in his acts. Therefore if he likes what his clients are doing he will charge nothing until the band are in a position to pay his fees when they make it. Oh, and Andrew doesn't actually wear a suit.

Ace from Skunk Anansie – even great musicians have to take care of business

Just sign here, here and here ...

So let's run through what it is that a band or an artist is agreeing to when they sign a recording deal, in layman's terms.

Rights

Effectively an artist or band are transferring the rights in their recordings that they make during a particular period. There are obviously all sorts of record deals, but the main type is along these lines; it's an exclusive deal, i.e. the band or artist cannot record for anyone else and whatever is recorded during that term is owned by the record company. A record deal is concerned with the rights in the performances, the rights in the recording.

It is important at this point to note that in a record there are two copyrights; there is the copyright in the performance or the recording, and there is the copyright in the composition which is embodied in the recording, i.e. publishing rights. What you are giving to the record company is the copyright in the recording. When you do a publishing deal you give the copyright in the composition to your publisher, but we'll deal with publishing later.

Once you give the recording rights over to a record company that company has the right, unless you ensure otherwise, to exploit the records in virtually any way. Andrew explains:

> 'Unless protection is built into the record contract on behalf of the band, they will not be able to stop any exploitation, for example their recording being included in a 'Tampon' advert or being re-mixed. Each band will have different concerns as to what happens to their recordings, and you take these into account when negotiating the deal. There are all sorts of approvals as to what a record company can and cannot do that you would hope to build in for a band. The rights are usually transferred in perpetuity under a recording deal, i.e. you don't get those rights back, the record company has them forever. But the record company should agree to pay you a royalty in respect of all exploitation. So for however long they exploit it, whenever money comes in, you get some of that money. The normal basis is that the record company pay the band's recording costs and a personal advance as well for the band to live on, but all those moneys become recoupable from your royalty at the end of the day.'

This is a very important point to note, that all moneys spent by the record company are recoupable, except for manufacturing, distribution and most marketing costs. There is a big difference between the terms 'recoupable' and 'repayable' because a record company can only recoup from moneys made from the product, i.e. sales of the record. Therefore it is in the band's interests to keep recording costs down so that the royalties will flow through that much quicker, and the band will put themselves in a much better position with regards the record company recouping their costs.

A record company cannot say 'we've given you this advance and you haven't had enough royalties to cover it, so we want our money back'. Having said that, most record companies do put in a right that if the band fails to deliver the product that it is meant to deliver, they can terminate the agreement and sue the band for the return of the advances. However although that clause will be in the contract somewhere, it is quite rare for a record company to use it. This is because it is very bad marketing for a record company to be seen to be suing one of their own artists.

INFO

*D*on't forget that all moneys spent by the record company are recoupable

Term

Another important aspect of a recording deal is the term of that deal. 'In a normal situation, you should be looking for at least a one album deal' explains Andrew,

'But hopefully the band can secure a two album 'firm' deal, where the record company will definitely make two albums. Usually though it's one album and the record company then takes four or five options for further albums. The important thing is that those are the record company's options, not the band's options. If the record company wants the band to make the record, the band is obliged to make the record. If the record company says that they don't want any more then that's it, the deal ends and the band is dropped.

So potentially these are very long term deals because if you said it was a deal for one album with four options, that's a possible five album deal. It can take over ten years to record five albums, so it is very important that the band know what they are getting into right from the start. They must be happy with the record company and know that this could be very long term, and that it is not up to them to get out of it. It could also be very short if the record company doesn't like the results, just one album.'

A lot of bands will come away from signing with a company saying 'yippee! We've just signed a six album deal!' and think that that is fantastic. Actually the more albums there are involved in the deal, the worse the case scenario is because it is the record company's options, it's up to them. It is therefore in the band's interest to keep the options as few as possible, because if the band is 'hot' a short deal means more possibilities of renegotiating or moving label for a greater return.

However with a major label who are investing all their money the band will be lucky to get a deal below one album plus four options. This is because they are investing all their money in the short term, so they are going to want to be sure that if and when the rewards come through, that they are in there for the long term to reap those rewards.

Advances

The advance obviously varies enormously depending on the size of the company, as a small independent just does not have the money to fund large advances, but in general with a major deal upwards of £100,000 is a reasonable starting point for a band. Sounds like a lot of money, doesn't it! Now imagine this: there are four members in your band and you have a manager. The manager will take 20 per cent straight away, so you are down to £80,000 before you have even started. So you have £80,000 to last your band approximately

18 months. It still sounds a lot, doesn't it? However if you then think of this as a yearly wage, it effectively amounts to between £13,000 and £14,000 a year. Unfortunately this only lasts for less than two years and then, unless you are selling records, you are penniless again! Do not forget that this only works out if you are extremely frugal, the minute you attempt any form of extravagance you're in trouble. It just is not enough to go away and live in the lap of luxury, which is where a lot of bands fall down. Andrew Myers makes the point:

> 'One of the first things I try and make very clear when bands sign a deal is that I want them to get involved with an accountant, who we can put them in touch with, and he can make a budget that works out exactly what they've got to spend each month taking into account the usual costs a new band faces. You find that a lot of bands go away and just spend all the money and then they come back to you a few months later and say 'its all gone'! However they don't get all the initial advance up front. Usually it's about 50 per cent on signature, another 25 per cent on commencement of recording and another 25 per cent on delivery of the recordings. So it can seem like quite a bit at first, but you realise when you break it down that there's not that much money there.'

If you get more than one label coming in for a band, then obviously it's much easier for a lawyer to negotiate. You could be looking at a £300,000 personal advance in respect of the first album, which is a nice hefty advance. But there are downsides to taking that big an advance because it puts a lot of pressure on the band. The record company will want quick results because it's spent a lot of money, and don't forget that there are recording costs on top of that. So you could be talking £300,000 personal advance against album one with recording costs of maybe £150,000, that's £450,000 unrecouped before you even think about videos.

The point is that with an advance this big, the band (and the record company) have got to have quite a big selling album to recoup that amount of money. If the album does not do well the record company will think very carefully before picking up the next option, because they will have to pay out another advance which will probably have to be more than the first.

It is a good idea therefore to keep the personal advances reasonable, because it will give the record company more opportunities to spend money on the things that really matter when it comes to promoting the album, like marketing, videos, recording costs and producers. These are the things that will actually make and promote the record in the first place, putting the band in a much better position to have success earlier and therefore reap the benefits in the long term. It is all a matter of making the most of your position and not going over the top.

Be aware!

It's happened before and, as sure as you are reading this book, it will happen again. It does not matter how streetwise a band may think they are, as soon as a record company waves a contract at them they go snow blind and run around in circles shouting 'yahoo'. A band should not get into the record contract at all. They can look at it, they can even have a read of it, but they should never try and negotiate it themselves. That is a big mistake. Any major record company will want the band to have an experienced music lawyer, because one of the ways that a band can challenge a record deal is if they have not had proper legal advice (in the court case between The Stone Roses and Silvertone, Clintons acted for The Stone Roses securing their release from their record deal). Indeed most good record deals will possess a clause in them instructing the artist to employ professional assistance.

It is also important that the band ensure that their legal representative places various restrictions on the use of their material, otherwise the record company can do whatever they like with the songs and the band can do nothing about it. How would you like the best song you have ever written to be used to advertise toilet roll or dog food? Another restriction should be placed upon the freedom to remix the band's music. Financially the costs of a remix are recoupable, but also a remix can have creative implications as it can make or break a track. Norman Cook usually turns a song into a hit when he remixes it, but this should be up to the band not the company.

Demos are another area that can lead to problems because unless you get a clause in the contract restricting their use, technically the record company could exploit your demos or outtakes. Obviously the band or artist did not intend these recording to be exploited, but the first draft of the contract will usually give these rights to the company unless there is a clause that says otherwise.

A first draft record deal will give the record company the right to do virtually whatever they want, it is therefore up to the band's legal representative to claw back the band's rights. Record companies are not trying to trick you, but they do produce a document which is clearly biased in their favour.

Do record companies still rip bands off?

So let's cut to the chase and ask that question that everybody wants to ask, do record companies still try and rip bands off? And if they do what can bands do about it? The simple answer to this is yes some record companies will try it on. The first thing is that a band should never ever sign anything without getting it seen by a lawyer first. Major labels will usually insist on dealing with a lawyer, they would not deal with the band directly. However it is the smaller record companies that a band may need to be wary of. A large percentage of them are bona fide companies who will be looking to complete a reasonable deal. But there are a small number of rogue companies out there that will try to turn a band over and make the most out of it, either through ignorance or by design, and it is this type of outfit that a band must be careful of.

How do you tell?

One of the easiest ways of telling is if they do not advise you to see a music lawyer, they just try to complete the deal. If this is happening to you, you can bet your musical future that the contract is going to contain a few clauses that a band will not want to be involved with.

It is all very well being able to sort out a few problems before the deal is done, but what happens if there is a legal dispute after the contract has been signed and what sort of problems can there be? This is, or should be, handled by a different department who will specialise in litigation, because this area is as vast a minefield as the commercial legal side. There can be all sorts of disputes regarding a band and the contract, for example when a band falls out with its record company because it is not doing its job properly – they are not putting the records out. If this happens then the lawyers may issue a writ or take other action that may lead to the termination of the record deal, but in some cases it may be that the band and the record company just fall out. There will be no actual breaches of contract that you could point to but there is no benefit in that band continuing to be signed to the company. At this point you just have to hope that the record company will be willing to settle the dispute and let the band go.

So what are the other common areas that can cause disputes?

'Other people infringing your client's rights' Andrew explains, 'be it bootleggers of records or merchandise, be it other bands performing using your name or one that is just too similar. There could be a tribute band who are marketing themselves in quite a dodgy way so that they don't come across as a tribute band. The other common one is libel and defamation, you know something in the newspaper that is inaccurate and untrue. Sometimes, of course, it's opinion and there is nothing you can do about it.

In a lot of minor label cases I may advise the artist to just walk away and ignore it because litigation is very negative, costly and basically if anything goes to court, it costs everyone a fortune and therefore it should be avoided. 95 per cent of cases that are started never end up in court, they are settled before that happens and a lot of litigators say that if you do end up in court, then you haven't done your job properly.

The other dispute that you often get is between managers and bands, if they can't work together then you have to find a way forward. It is usually in the manager's interest to have a contract to ensure that he or she is in there for a term, i.e. he or she will be managing the band for a set period. With managers you usually find there is a dispute when the manager is a mate who has been acting for the band initially, and then the band realise that their mate is just not up to the job. At that point they decide that to get some success they will have to get a top manager in to move the band on from doing OK to doing fantastic.'

Let's do a publishing deal

It is important here to distinguish between who represents who and what. Publishers represent the writer of a song and the song itself, while record companies represent the recorded artist and the recording of the song. If Whitney Houston is advised that she would have a massive hit with a particular song written by someone else, then Whitney and her recording of the song are represented by the record company. The actual song itself and the writer of the song are protected by the publishing company. This independence between the two has become an added way of protecting artists who also write their own songs, ensuring that the record company do not have a hold over every aspect of an artist's career. For example if a record company owned the publishing rights to a writer/artist's songs it is possible that they could shelve the artist, thus ruining his or her career, whilst still having open access to their songs.

When a writer of a song signs a publishing deal two things happen, firstly there is a 'transfer of title' where the writer loses control of the song, secondly the publishers collect all of the income generated by the song and retain for themselves a share of around 20 – 30 per cent, so why sign a publishing deal? Basically most musicians are not very good at business and so do not understand or know how to protect and exploit the potential of their song.

Publishers will pay the writer/band an advance which is recoupable, they have the contacts within the music business to exploit songs and they know how to exploit a song to its best potential. They will provide administration services such as the registration of the song with the Performing Right Society and the Mechanical Copyright Protection Society, who both collect moneys on behalf of their members, and the publisher ensures the collection and distribution of royalties from these societies and provide the writer with legal protection.

Publishers are able to negotiate large sums of money for songs for their use in films and adverts for example, and they have the means and the knowledge to protect the copyright, i.e. to ensure that the work is not infringed or used without permission.

INFO

A case in point was the relationship between the Stone Roses and their record company, Silvertone Records. Via the recording contract, Silvertone had acquired the publishing rights to all the Stone Roses' songs amongst other limiting contractual agreements. The Stone Roses eventually managed to take Silvertone to court (with Clintons help) and the final ruling found against Silvertone for 'unjustifiable restraint of trade'.

Ultimately however most writers sign a deal to receive another advance.

A publishing deal, like a recording deal, is usually exclusive so anything you write during the term of the deal will be passed to the publishing company. Also anything that you have written prior to the term, unless you had a previous publishing deal, will get passed to the publishing company. One big difference between this and a recording deal is that you will usually agree a rights period, after which the rights in those songs will be returned. So if you want to do another deal afterwards, you can, or you can keep hold of them. The length of that period is down to negotiation, but it is in the publishers interests to make it around 15 years while you will want it to be no more than five, so you will settle somewhere in the middle.

The term is very similar to a recording deal in that they will probably do it over a one album period with three options, so what ever you write during that period goes to them. You will be under a commitment to get one album released which will contain a certain amount of material which has been written by you, and you will receive an advance against that happening. The important thing to remember here is that it is the writer of the songs who will sign up to this, not the whole band, unless of course the whole band have writing input. The publishing company then have the right to exploit those songs in anyway that they see fit, so if you want to restrict those rights you must make sure that they are built into the contract, or it's too late.

What's a publishing deal worth?

Let's get technical for a minute, because it pays to know these things, and have a quick look at rates of pay from publishing deals. The rate will differ from deal to deal but what you should be looking for with a major company is an 'at source' deal. With this you will get a share of all moneys that arise from your material at source, and not those received, so there are no sub-publisher deductions taken off. Smaller publishing companies will have to go through a sub-publisher (explained in a second!) and so you will get a 'net receipts deal'.

What this means is say £100 arises from one of your songs in America, the sub-publisher that your publishing company have employed to work for them over the pond take 20 per cent, so £80 comes back to your publisher in Britain and then that is split in accordance with your agreement. So if you agree a 75-25 'net receipts' split you will get £60, whereas with an 'at source' deal you would have ended up with £75. And that's it!

Andrew's advice column

1 Do record a demo tape of no more than three songs, and make sure the quality is as reasonable as possible.

2 If you can, make sure that your tape is not unsolicited, i.e. make sure it arrives on the A&R person's desk via a reputable route like a lawyer or a manager. It is not worth just sending them a tape and hoping for the best. Don't forget that Andrew and his associates are always happy to have a listen to your new demos!

3 A band should (depending on the style of music) be gigging and their live performance should be consummately professional.

4 Only start gigging in London when the band is truly ready.

5 Be patient. It takes time to get to a stage where a band is close to doing a deal, and to getting the right sort of deal. It helps when doing a deal to have a few record labels chasing you, and it is in the band's best interests to build to this stage rather than take the first deal that comes along.

6 At an early stage a band should get involved with a good manager and a good lawyer because both of these people can be getting the name of your band into the right places.

7 You never have a contract with a lawyer, therefore even if a band does make it with a particular lawyer's help it does not mean that they have to be represented by him or her in the future.

8 Avoid lawyers who try to take a percentage, because that does not necessarily work out in the interest of the band. Most lawyers charge on a time basis, so get an estimate.

9 Remember! Cheaper is not always better and less qualified lawyers charge lesser rates (think of it in the same way as hiring an electrician). Find a lawyer with good experience who is prepared to be flexible with his/her fees in the early days.

Business structure

All professional projects should be structured into a defined business format and given their own identity. Various forms of business structure exist and the right one for your project is individual to it. When you sign a major recording contract you will be wise to employ the services of a specialised music business accountant. These services will be expensive, but it is vital that all areas of income and expense are accounted for accurately, and presented in a way that makes sense to the tax man. During the course of this chapter we're going to be taking a look at three of the most common ways to structure a business in the early days, and these are as follows:

- Sole traderships
- Partnerships
- Limited companies

Sole traderships

What is a sole trader?

Becoming a sole trader is as easy as the name suggests, it simply means someone that has decided to go into business for themselves. If you're a solo artist you should formalise yourself as a business (sole trader) as this gives the whole project an independent and professional feel and also puts a physical and

TIP

Make sure that you go round all the high street banks searching for the best deal and remember that you are the customer. Many banks offer free start up packs for small businesses which are extremely informative.

physiological distance between your professional and personal life. OK so what's involved.

- Well first of all you open a bank account in the name of your business e.g. Matey Boy Music. All business cheques and correspondence will read 'Your name' trading as 'Matey Boy Music'.
- Secondly you need to register as self employed with the Inland Revenue.
- Thirdly you need to register with the DSS for National Insurance contributions.

That's it!

One optional extra that I would recommend is that you find an accountant that can teach you simple bookkeeping and help you with your end of year tax return. There's hundreds of accountants out there, go and see at least three and if they won't give you a half hour free consultation then forget it. Go with your instincts, if they seem to take a genuine interest in your project/s then give them a try.

Before you start out, open a high interest savings account and put 25 per cent of your earnings into it. Many self employed people forget this and then have a real hard time dealing with their first tax bill a year down the line. If you put your tax contribution away each month at least you earn the interest. Your accountant will be able to advise you on how much you can earn before you have to worry about paying tax. This is called your personal allowance and sadly it is not very much! Again, this does not sound very rock'n'roll, but you do want to make a living, right?

It pays to be self employed –
Keith Richards
Pic courtesy Duncan Raban

Never underestimate the power of the taxman. Most musicians have tales of woe in this area. Bruce Dickinson had a narrow escape when his band split up in 1994 ...

'When we split the band we thought we'd be okay financially. I mean there was 100k in the band account. We thought that by the time we'd paid off a few debts there would be at least 10k each left, which would tide us over until we figured out what we were going to do with the rest of our lives. Unfortunately when you shut down a company you get clobbered for two years tax because you're paying in arrears until the point that you try and shut the thing down when the tax man gets last year's tax and this year's all at once. The upshot was that we ended up with a grand each after eight year's work, 14 hit singles and a number one album. To add insult to injury we were taxed on that grand the following year! At that point I realised how useful a good accountant can be. A really serious operator can get you out of all sorts of trouble and save a lot of money.'

Partnerships

A partnership is the same as a sole tradership in that the people are the business. The difference is that there is more than one person involved. Partnerships don't necessarily have to be made up of only two people they can represent however many are involved in the project. If you're in a band then this type of business structure may be appropriate.

It's not too complicated, in fact it's exactly the same as for a sole trader except you have more arguments! It is easy to form a partnership but can be harder and costlier to dissolve it.

If you have a partner who owns one third of the partnership for example, just because you may fall out and sack that musician from the band does not mean that you can sack them from the partnership. They own a third and you may be faced with the very real possibility of having to buy them out at full market price. Many projects are very careful about exactly which band members are in or out of the partnership. Musicians who join established projects are rarely allowed to join the elite partners, usually merely being employed by the partnership as a glorified session musician.

Limited company

The difference between this business structure and the sole trader and partnership arrangements is that the limited company is an entity in its own right. So if you were to build your projects into this type of business structure it means that the company would employ you and the other band members and any profit/loss would be

TIP

*I*f you're formalising your band project as a partnership then ensure that every detail to do with finance is topped and tailed before you set off on the road to stardom. This type of business structure is really flexible so if it's appropriate for the writer to have a greater percentage of the business then that's OK but put it in writing.

attributed according the initial percentage of shares agreed upon at its inception. Most pro bands are structured in this format with the band members being company shareholders. The fun begins when one band member considers that they contribute just that little bit more that the other members and so deserves a greater shareholding. Here's where the manager comes in! The best way to resolve these types of disputes is to agree the band politics before you start out. Once again there are loads of ways to structure the shares but they all tend to boil down to one of two options:

- Democracy (equal shareholding between band members, equal rights, voting and those kinds of things)
- Dictatorship (one member with majority of shares, casting vote, everyone does what they say and are more like hired guns)

Either of these solutions works as long as the lines are clearly drawn in the sand. The limited company option is normally only entertained as an artist or band is being signed i.e. gearing up for an infusion of cash. Most people feel secure dealing with a company that has limited in the title. Ironically a limited company means that the shareholders have limited liability so if it goes bust creditors (people that it owes money to) cannot pursue the shareholders personal assets for outstanding monies.

Creating a business plan

Regardless of the business structure that's most appropriate to your situation as an artist the most important thing to sort out is the business plan. Most new businesses see writing a business plan as an exercise for trusts or the bank, however if it's meaningful, it can act as a blueprint for the entire project and its development. In Chapter 2 we looked at the mapping, planning and practical outworking of products, marketing, teamwork and time/project management.

The business plan gives an overview of the project objectives, how they will be achieved and the financial implications associated with the business and its development. Many bands ignore their responsibilities in the area of business planning and leave the hard work to the manager, concentrating on the music only. Whilst this is an acceptable situation, if your manager is a good one, it does put your future in the hands of other people. It is interesting to note that most artists who are around for the long term in the business take a very 'hands on' approach to business planning.

Writing the plan

Overview

Outlined below are the main topic headings you should be considering for the business plan. Your business plan should give a clear and concise explanation of how you expect to initiate and go onto complete your first 12 months' trading. It should include a full financial breakdown (month by month) ending with a prediction of how much money you will end up with at the end of the first 12 months.

Many bands find that a 12 month period allows them to realistically plan for and target a major record deal. Of course if a deal comes earlier than expected so much the better, but many musicians are surprised how long it takes the lawyers and management to agree the small print before the contract is actually signed. Even if you were offered a deal after only six months activity it could be a full 12 months before advances were forthcoming.

Structure

You will need to include certain categories or headings to ensure that you capture all the relevant information. This is a standard business plan for a small business that we will adapt for a rock 'n' roll band:

Business plan

About the business:

This section deals with the artist/band name, products to be sold and the mission statement.

Market research and marketing:

Here you'll be dealing with who's going to buy your products (music, merchandise and videos etc,) the marketplace, competition etc.

Promotions and advertising:

Analysis of how you intend to inform your potential fans that you exist and have a product/s that they need to take a look at.

Business location:

Identification of the most appropriate premises and area for your band to be based.

Personnel:

Who's going to run the band and justification of their ability to do so.

Future planning:

Expansion plan for 24, 36 and 48 months.

Costing:

Analysis of the initial set up costs and potential income (if any)

Cashflow forecast:

Monthly breakdown of the business income/expenditure for the first year.

Profit and loss:

Analysis of the business performance at the end of 12 months trading.

Pro tips

- Always write in the third party
- Never repeat the same word in a sentence or start consecutive sentences with the same word.
- Keep your statements concise
- Ensure that each section consolidates the position of the previous one and that all figures and financial statements make sense.
- Present the plan as a professionally bound document
- Demonstrate initiative throughout
- Support all ideas and concepts with factual evidence.
- Keep the presentation visually exciting and easy to comprehend

The purpose of writing this plan is to consolidate and focus your thinking on the project. Writing the plan will expose any woolly ideas or naive assumptions that the act may be labouring under. Of course you're not going to present this plan to a bank manager but you may run it past a manager. As Kevin Nixon says:

> 'It's so great when I come across a good band with a sense of direction and a plan. It makes it easier for me, as a manager, to help them realise their aims. How they articulate that vision doesn't really matter it could be on paper or in a verbal statement. If its focused and realistic then that's a great start ...'

If we were to follow the rather rigid structure for writing a standard business plan we might be considering the following points: Before commencing a business plan we need to choose an appropriate name for the project. When doing this we need to be very careful that the name is versatile enough to allow for development but specific enough to link your product or service with the relevant area of the marketplace. Many new artists/acts shoot themselves in the foot by choosing a name that restricts future development e.g. bands with the name 'Death' in the title. Ironically this 'limiting factor ' may just be the thing to springboard a new band into a specific market. If the market is big enough it won't necessarily be a problem that future developments are restricted. The pros and cons of a non-specific or specific name need to be thought about very carefully because it is almost impossible to change a name once the act becomes established. Sound familiar? That's because we've already discussed these points in Chapter 1. You thought we were coming up with a cool band name when actually we were working towards making a cool business plan too.

Once you've established your name you need to think about your logo. This needs to have effective visual impact, be instantly recognisable and must be able to be used in a variety of different forms e.g. letterheads, album covers etc. Think of companies that offer products and bands that you recognise simply from seeing their Logo. A good logo can generate all kinds of interest in the band. Bruce Dickinson remembers the mileage his old band got out of a cartoon logo of a devil.

'We had a young audience and they really adopted the devil logo. Kids liked to draw it on school bags and I think it gave them a sense of 'belonging to the club' if they had a T-shirt with the devil on. The character became notorious after a while because the artist, Charlie Cutforth, had cleverly added in extra subliminal graphics. If you looked carefully at the devil's eyebrows and bridge of the nose, you could see a huge phallus penetrating female sexual organs. Once you could see it the obscene image was very obvious and caused great controversy amongst the fans (and their parents). After that every T-shirt had to have a subliminal design hidden in it. The shirts became collector's items as a result and of course we sold a lot of them.'

The Little Angels devil logo – the fans loved it and bought the T-shirt

Your 'mission statement' should describe in a sentence exactly what it is that you aim to achieve with the band. Someone that knows nothing about your music should be able to comprehend exactly what the act's objectives are simply by reading the mission statement. This means that at any one time you can look back on the mission statement to assess whether you are achieving your initial vision or failing in your primary aims. For a rock 'n' roll band a mission statement should detail the direction of the project and who is going to buy the product.

For both yourself and the reader it is imperative that you identify exactly what it is you're selling. You should describe in clearly defined terms how you're going to create the music and image and give details of any unique selling points (USP's). USP's are any unique points that make your act stand out from the competition. Often people establishing a new business go overboard looking for a brand new product or service, however most strokes of genius occur when an entrepreneur simply adds a twist to a product or service that already exists thus making it appear fresh to the customer. Many huge rock and pop acts are not wildly original, simply adding a new spin on tried and tested formulas.

So when designing this page follow these points:

- Keep it simple
- Be precise
- Don't be too technical

It goes without saying that all business plans are word processed but for extra visual impact use a simple desk top publishing package.

Market research and marketing

Once you've established your product or service, in our case a 'look' and a 'sound' it's very important to link it to a specific group or type of record buyer. So many young bands fail in this area through an over belief in their product coupled with a naivety of their market. Avoid the following examples:

People will buy it from me because they buy it from him
Many bands go down this route of assumption, be careful ! Another act may already have the lion's share of the market. It is difficult to establish a new product alongside this type of business. e.g. Imagine a small business launching their own brand of ketchup against Heinz. You would need very strong USP's to convince their customers to buy/try your product, not to mention convincing the shops to retail the product in the first place. It would be extremely naive for a band to assume that just because Bon Jovi offer a certain type of music, and are successful in doing so, it would be realistic for another project to be able to do something similar and attract even a small portion of that audience. Another area to be careful of is the location for which you're targeting your product/service. Just because someone is selling an amazing amount of records in the UK doesn't mean that you will able to do the same in America.

So how do you establish where, when and how much ? Firstly take a close look at your competitors. Whilst it would be ridiculous to assume that simply because they're successful you'll be successful you can learn a great deal from them. For example: how much they charge, where they advertise, their image, the structure of their products. When analysing this information be subjective.

Many new businesses and bands often seem too self assured, assuming that their products or services are far superior to the competition that may have been successful for years! This attitude can often lead to disaster, listen carefully and learn from as many different sources as you can. Most importantly identify your client. Gain as much information on them as you can e.g. gender, social

Have you seen this man somewhere before?

stature, income bracket, age group, other pursuits, etc. In addition to this you will need to establish whether they're interested in your product. This needs to be hard fact. Many new bands commence their careers believing that their fan base is one type of person and then end up selling to a different group altogether, making the job of marketing the act inefficient. More usually, the band are aiming for a market that doesn't exist or is already saturated and dominated by established acts.

The term 'promotions and advertising' is often confused with marketing. The two should be clearly defined as follows: marketing can be described as the linking of specific products to the relevant areas of the marketplace, and promotions and advertising are the various media used to create public awareness of the availability of your products. When discussing your promotions and advertising programme it's important that you are seen to be creative. Of course if and when you sign a record deal, the record company itself may take up the responsibility for this area of the plan. Until that point you will be looking after your own promotions and having to make the most of every opportunity. You need to make it clear to the reader exactly where you are going to advertise and why, making sure that all reasoning is strongly supported by the market research and the marketing section of the plan.

Designing a demo pack and other promotional materials

When discussing the type of materials that you are going to use to represent your band you need to be clear on how they will specifically relate to your target market, here are some design guidelines relevant to all age groups and most products:

- Keep all information simple and user friendly, remember people will give up if it looks like hard work.
- Establish a strong identity from the outset so that your advertising, posters, flyers, brochure, letterheads all tie in with each other and the image that you're creating.
- Give maximum shelf life to all your long term promotional materials by keeping 'variables' (dates etc.) on a separate 'in house' sheet.

During this section of the business plan it would be good to generate some visuals using a simple desktop publishing package.

Personnel

At some point you may decide to include a business/company structure which would simply include a graph outlining the different tasks to be achieved and whose responsible for what. Each position may also be tagged with a pay band indicating the lowest and highest salary payable for each position. Keep this graph impersonal i.e. don't include any names simply give the job titles. Outlined below is an illustration of how this could look:

Pay bands

Band 1	Directors
Band 2	Manager
Band 3	Sound Man, Session Musicians
Band 4	Roadies, Drivers, Tour Manager, Bookkeeper, Accountant

Pay band 1	Salary agreed by directors (usually the band themselves)
Pay band 2	Usually 20 per cent of gross income
Pay band 3	Daily rate plus possible retainer
Pay band 4	Daily rate negotiated at interview

Company structure

This structure is very useful for you to gain a specific understanding of how you visualise your business running and then offer assistance in areas that may be lacking. Avoid the classic mistake of writing a particular person into a job rather than analysing the specific job that needs to be fulfilled and then interviewing to find the most qualified candidate. Many bands employ their mates and relatives when they begin to be successful – this invariably leads to problems later on.

Future developments

This section of the business plan is like a memo pad for both yourself and the reader to assess the future potential of the band. The key to a strong business is that each new venture strengthens the existing projects quickly and effectively. Once established, an effectively managed project should be able to expand and contract, quickly modifying itself to the marketplace and audience requirements, whilst at the same time channelling its clients from one product to the next.

Our clients are our fan base, and our products are singles, albums, merchandise and videos. You need to give the reader the impression that the sky is the limit with regard to your business plan. However, should a project fail or meet with a less than expected response, you must be able to demonstrate that you have various contingency plans for moving quickly in an adapted or new direction.

The following areas of the business plan are probably the most crucial and will determine whether you will be able to secure loans and other sources of finance against the project.

> **TIP**
>
> *B*e realistic in your aims and objectives but at the same time be creative, spend time thinking about new products and concepts that will strengthen your existing position in the marketplace.

Set up costs and necessary equipment

Under this sub heading you should include all your set up costs from raw materials to promotional materials from telecommunications to transport, in other words everything you need in order to commence trading. Give accurate costings for all items, individually labelled.

Once you've established exactly what equipment you need and how much it will cost you need to give clarification of where the finance will come from to back it. If you are sending the business plan out with a view to receiving backing you need to give specific indication of what items you require financial assistance with.

Costing

Under this sub heading you need to give clear indication of the retail prices of your product or service, margin per cent, monthly income (broken down by product/service if you intend to offer more than one) and then balance this with your out goings giving a specific break even point.

In the early days of a band's career income will come from gig fees and merchandise. This you do by listing your expenses as shown below:

Categories	Weekly estimate	Monthly estimate	Quarterly estimate	Annual budget
Salaries				
Transport				
Rehearsal costs				
Recording costs				
Equipment				
Legal fees				
Advertising				
Design, printing, stationery				
Postage				
Accountancy				
Bookkeeping				
Insurance				
Drawings				
Misc.				

Multiply weekly items by 52, monthly ones by 12 and quarterly ones by 4 (as appropriate). Now you should have an annual total for all expenses. Add these together and divide by 48 (not 52) to allow for holidays. The resulting figure is what you need to earn each week to break even.

To take things a stage further you could divide this figure by the number of hours you intend to work each week e.g. 40 (realistically more like 90!) and you will achieve your basic hourly rate. If this rate seems ludicrous then you need to re-think the plan, if not then you have solid financial criteria upon which to proceed. Your first year's cashflow forecast will serve to underline the point that starting a serious project will require a considerable investment of time, effort and money for little short term gain.

This section of the business plan provides you with your financial roadmap for a full 12 month period and follows the following format:

	April Budget	Actual	May Budget	Actual	June Budget	Actual	July Budget	Actual
Receipts								
Record Advances								
Publishing advances								
Royalties (recording, mechanicals, PRS etc)								
Merchandising advances								
Tour profits								
Capital introduced								
Total receipts (a)								
Payments								
Salaries								
Rehearsal costs								
Equipment								
Transport								
Design, printing								
Postage, stationery								
Accountancy								
Bookkeeping								
Insurance								
Capital payments								
Interest charges								
Drawings								
Misc.								
Other								
Total payments (b)								
Net cashflow (a-b)								
Opening bank balance								
Closing bank balance								

Obviously this example covers only four months, however it demonstrates the principle. The important thing to remember is that a cashflow forecast is an attempt to predict your cashflow situation over 12 months and it is for this reason that income and expenditure must be entered under the appropriate month, e.g. a healthy bank balance at the end of month 3 does not mean you can have a spending spree in month 4 as your cashflow budget will remind you that all your quarterly bills are due.

Each of the main items of income and expenditure should be explained in an appendix to the cashflow entitled 'Cashflow notes'. Ensure that all finance data is logical and easy to follow.

Profit and loss

The profit and loss account gives a summary of how financially successful you think you will be at the end of one year's trading. It is laid out as below:

Sales (a)	£
Less direct (variable) costs (b)	£
Gross profit (a-b) = c	£
Fixed costs	
Salaries	£
Rehearsal costs	£
Transport	£
Postage, stationery	£
Accountancy	£
Bookkeeping	£
Insurance	£
Capital payments	£
Interest charges	£
Total fixed costs (d)	£
Total taxable profits (c-d)	£
Less tax (don't forget personal allowances)	£
Drawings	£
Retained in business	£

Notes

> • Direct costs – the variable costs that relate directly to sales volume, when deducted from sales this gives what is known as the 'Gross Profit'.
> • Fixed costs can be categorised as costs you need to pay regardless of how much you sell. When deducted from the gross profit gives you your taxable profit.
> • Notice that your drawings are not classed a fixed cost, these are considered part of the taxable profit and will be taxed at the appropriate rate.

It is up to you to decide how involved you want to get in the financial management of the project. Many musicians find it hard to be creative when they have a head full of figures and cashflow forecasts. On the other hand it's hard to be creative if you're going bankrupt! At the very least it is hoped that this chapter has given you enough information to ask meaningful questions of your accountant and not feel too intimidated in the presence of the money men.

12 Useful addresses and phone numbers

Being able to contact the right person at the right time is absolutely imperative in the music business, and to be able to do this you must have two things: the confidence to contact them in the first place, and their address and telephone number.

The confidence to phone up and make that connection can come from various sources. Believing in yourself and your music is always a good start, but on a more simplistic level it is good to remember that the chances are the person on the other end of the line is waiting for someone like you to call. Remember not all music professionals are cynical old goats, mostly they are people trying to do a good job of work. This is the main reason why they always seem to be busy when you call, it is not because they are trying to avoid you! Do not be put off by being told that he or she is in a meeting, because they probably are. Just make sure that you leave your name and tell them that you will phone them back, and make sure that you do. Do not rely on them phoning you because they probably won't.

So who is it that you are going to contact? Well that is down to you, but remember that record companies can be defined just like bands. So do some research, and if you are an acoustic folk duo do not bother sending a tape to Dan at Earache Records!

What you will find below is a list of useful contacts for various important areas of the music world. There are record companies, music papers and magazines, solicitors and accountants. Also included are some useful contacts for official bodies and professional help. This is not a comprehensive list, as the music industry is always changing, it is just a starting point.

Record companies

3rd Stone Records Ltd
PO Box 8
Corby NN17 1XZ
Tel: 01536 202295
Fax: 01536 266246

A New Day
75 Wren Way
Farnborough
Hampshire GU14 8TA
Tel: 01252 540270
Fax: 01252 372001

A&M Records
136-144 New Kings Road
London SW6 4LZ
Tel: 020 7705 4343
Fax: 020 7731 4606

Ace Records Ltd
42-50 Steele Road
London NW10 7AS
Tel: 020 8453 1311
Fax: 020 896 18725

Alpha Records Ltd
1, Abbey Street
Eynsham
Oxford OX8 1HR
Tel: 01865 880240

AnXious Records
The Electric Lighting Station
46, Kensington Court
London W8 5DP
Tel: 020 7938 2181
Fax: 020 7937 6645

Art and Soul Records Ltd
Burlington House
64, Chiswick High Road
London W4 1SY
Tel: 020 8742 3366
Fax: 020 8742 3311

Badlands
11 St Georges Place
Cheltenham GL50 3LA
Tel: 01242 227724
Fax: 01242 227393

Barracuda Blue Records
Barracuda House
42 Gibbon Road
Newhaven
Sussex BN9 9EP
Tel: 01273 513288

Beat Goes On Records
7, St Andrews Street North
Bury St Edmunds IP33 1TZ
Tel: 01284 762137
Fax: 01284 762433

Big Bang Records
PO Box 15053
Glasgow G2 4YH
Tel: 0141 248 3637
Fax: 0141 248 3667

Big Moon Records
PO Box 347
Weybridge
Surrey KT13 9WZ
Tel: 01932 859472
Fax: 01932 889802

BMG
Bedford House
69-70 Fulham High Street
London SW6 3JW
Tel: 020 7384 7500
Fax: 020 7371 9298

Bomba Records
16-20 Hope Street
Glasgow
Strathclyde G2 6AA
Tel: 0141 248 8831
Fax: 0141 248 5888

Breakin Loose
32 Quadrant House
Burrell Street
London SE1 0UW
Tel: 020 7633 9576

Cargo Records
The Studio, Edith Villas
Bective Road
London SW5 2QA
Tel: 020 8875 9220
Fax: 020 88759227

Champion Records
181 High Street
Harlesden
London NW10 4TE
Tel: 020 8961 5202
Fax: 020 8965 3948

China Records
111, Frithville Gardens
London W12 7JG
Tel: 020 8742 9999
Fax:020 8742 9942/9353

Chrysalis Records Ltd
EMI House
43, Brook Green
London W6 7EF
Tel: 020 7605 5000
Fax: 020 7605 5050

Cooking Vinyl
3, Park Mews
213, Kilburn Lane
London W10 4BQ
Tel: 020 8960 6000
Fax: 020 8960 1120

Creation Records
109x Regents Park Road
London NW1 8UR
Tel: 020 7722 8866
Fax: 020 7722 3443

Cutting Edge Music
20 Accommodation Rd
London NW11 8EP
Tel: 020 8455 5560
Fax: 020 8455 5355

Defunkt Records
1 Constance Street
Knott Hill
Manchester M15 4PS
Tel: 0161 236 6616
Fax: 0161 228 2399

Demon Records Ltd
Canal House
Stars Estate
Transport Ave
Brentford TW8 9HF
Tel: 020 8847 2481

DG Records
5, Paddington Street
London W1M 3LA
Tel: 020 7935 1588
Fax: 020 7487 3016

Distinctive
Berners House
1st Floor
47-48 Berners St
London W1
Tel: 020 7323 6610

Donut
111 The Business Design Centre
52 Upper Street
London N1 0QH
Tel: 020 7288 6048
Fax: 020 7288 6047

Dragon Records
5 Church Street
Aylesbury
Buckinghamshire HP20 2QP
Tel: 01296 415333

EG Records Ltd
63a Kings Road
London SW3 4NT
Tel: 020 7730 2162
Fax: 020 7730 1330

Earache Records Ltd
Suite 1-3
Westminster Building
Theatre Square
Nottingham NG1 6LG
Tel: 0115 950 6400

Eagle Records
Eagle House
22 Armoury Way
London SW18 1EZ
Tel: 020 8870 5670
Fax: 020 8875 0050

East West Records Ltd
The Electric Lighting Station
46, Kensington Court
London W8 5DP
Tel: 020 7938 2181
Fax: 020 7937 6645

EMI Records
43, Brook Green
London W6 7EF
Tel: 020 7605 5000
Fax: 020 7605 5050

Egg Records
1 Hesketh Street
Liverpool
Merseyside L17 8XJ
Tel: 0151 727 75577
Fax: 0151 283 3649

Eye Q
8-9 Rivington Place
London WC2A 3BA
Tel: 020 7739 1231
Fax: 020 7385 6785

Factory Records
2-4 Little Peter Street
Manchester M15 4PS
Tel: 0161 834 4440
Fax: 0161 834 4700

Fiction Records Ltd
4, Tottenham Mews
London W1P 9PJ
Tel: 020 7323 5555
Fax: 020 7323 5323

Fly Records
11, Uxbridge Street
London W8 7QT
Tel: 020 7221 4275
Fax: 020 7229 6893

Flying Rhino Records
252, Belsize Road
London NW6 4BT
Tel: 020 7624 8555
Fax: 020 7624 8027

Food Records Ltd
9, Greenland Street
Camden
London NW1 0ND
Tel: 020 7284 2554
Fax: 020 7284 2560

Fragile Records Ltd
9, Hillgate Street
London W8 7SP
Tel: 020 7727 2791
Fax: 020 7243 8548

Gammer Records
39, Ivygreen Road
Chorlton-Cum-Hardy
Gtr Manchester
Tel: 0161 860 4133

Gimmell Records Ltd
4, Newtec Place
Magdalen road
Oxford OX4 1RE
Tel: 01865 244557
Fax: 01865 790472

Go. Beat
1st Fleet, Bond House
347-353,Chiswick
High Road,
London W4 4HS
Tel: 020 8910 4600
Fax: 020 8742 5575

Gut Records Ltd
Bryon House
112a, Shirland Road
London W9 2EQ
Tel: 020 7266 0777
Fax: 020 7266 1293

Hands on Records Ltd
3, Lambton Place
London W11 2SH
Tel: 020 7221 7872
Fax: 020 7221 7195

Hardware Records
2nd Floor
Half Moon Chambers
Bigg Market
Newcastle-Upon-Tyne NE1 1UW
Tel: 0191 233 0899
Fax: 0191 233 0834

Instant Karma Records
36 Sackville Street
London W1X 1DB

Indolent Records
69-79 Fulham High
Street
London SW6 3JW
Fax: 020 7973 0332

Iona Records
27-29 Carnoustie Place
Scotland Street
Glasgow
Strathclyde
Tel: 0141 420 1881
Fax: 0141 420 1892

Island Records Ltd
22, St Peters Square
London W6 9NW
Tel: 020 8910 3333
Fax: 020 8748 1998

Jazz Fudge Records
6 Lenelby Road
Tolworth
Surbiton
Surrey KT6 7BH
Tel: 020 8390 0805
Fax: 020 8287 7363

Jelly Street Records Ltd
Grosvenor House
94-96 Grosvenor Street
Manchester M1 7HL
Tel: 0161 273 6522
Fax: 0161 273 6592

Killerwatt Records
61 Collier Street
London N1 9BE
Tel: 020 7713 7788
Fax: 020 7713 0099

Kingsize Records
28-30 High Street
Weybridge
Surrey KT13 8AB
Tel: 01932 831053
Fax: 01932 827571

Kudos Records
Unit 1, Canada House
Blackburn Road
London NW6 1RZ
Tel: 020 7372 0391
Fax: 020 7372 0392

Lager Records
62 Lytton Ave
Letchworth
Hertfordshire SG6 3HU
Tel: 01462 623552

Launchpad Music UK
8 Emmbrook Road
Wokingham
Berkshire RG41 1HE
Tel: 0118 978 5138
Fax: 0118 979 9989

Loaded
PO Box 174
Brighton
East Sussex BN1 4BA
Tel: 01273 738527
Fax: 01273 208766

London Records 90 Ltd
PO Box 1422
Chancellors House
Chancellors Road
London W6 9SG
Tel: 020 8910 5111
Fax: 020 8910 5907

Magnet Records Ltd
The Warner Building
28, Kensington Church Street
London W8 4EP
Tel: 020 7937 8844
Fax: 020 7937 6645

Manchester Underground
Recordings
33 Fennel Street
Manchester M4 3DY
Tel: 0161 839 4043

MAP
27 Abercorn Place
London NW8 9DX
Tel: 0374 267373
Fax: 020 7624 7219

Mercury
PO Box 1425,
Chancellors House
Chancellors Road
London W6 9QB
Tel: 020 8910 5678
Fax: 020 8910 5896

Mushroom Records Ltd
1, Shorrolds Road
London SW6 7TR
Tel: 020 7343 5678
Fax: 020 7343 5656

Music For Nations Ltd
333, Latimer Road
London W10 6RA
Tel: 020 8964 9544
Fax: 020 8964 5460

Mute Records
429 Harrow Road
London W10 4RE
Tel: 020 89698 866
Fax: 020 8968 4977

Nation Records
19 All Saints Road
London W11 1HE
Tel: 020 7792 8167
Fax: 020 7792 2854

Neat Records
71 High Street East
Wallsend
Tyne and Wear NE28 7RJ
Tel: 0191 262 4999
Fax: 0191 263 7082

Nimbus Records
Wyastone Leys
Monmouth
Gwent NP5 3SR
Tel: 01600 890682
Fax: 01600 890779

Nervous Records
7-11 Minerva Road
London NW10 6HJ
Tel: 020 8963 0352
Fax: 020 8963 1170

Polydor Ltd
72, Black Lion Lane
Hammersmith
London W6 9BE
Tel: 020 8910 4800
Fax: 020 8910 4801

Polygram
(now Universal Music)
PO Box 1420
1 Sussex Place
London W6 9XS
Tel: 020 8910 5000
Fax: 020 8741 4901

Red Dragon Records Ltd
SF House
48, Cottage Road
Leeds
LS6 4DD
Tel: 0113 293 0101

RoadRunner Records Ltd
Suites Wand T
Tech West Centre 10
Warple Way
London W3 0UL
Tel: 020 8749 2948
Fax: 020 8749 2523

Sony 2
10 Great Malborough Street
London W1V 2LP
Tel: 020 7911 8200
Fax: 020 7911 8600

Splash Records
Manor House
29 Marylebone Rd
London NW1 5NP
Tel: 020 7723 7177

Transient Records
129 Canalot Studios
222 Kensall Road
London W10 5BN
Tel: 020 8964 8890
Fax: 020 8960 5741

Universal Music
1 Sussex Place
London W6 9XS
Tel: 020 8910 5000
Fax: 020 8741 4901

Utopia Records
7 Chalcot Road
London NW1 8LH
Tel: 020 7586 3434

V2 Records
131-133 Holland Park Avenue
London W11 4UT
Tel: 020 7471 3000

WEA Records
The Warner Building
28 Kensington Church St
London W8 4EP
Tel: 020 7937 8844

Music solicitors

Clintons (Andrew Myers)
55 Drury Lane
London WC2B 5SQ
Tel: 020 7379 6080

Harbottle and Lewis (Andy Stinson)
14 Hanover Square
London W1R 0BE
Tel: 020 7667 5000

Stratham Gill Davies (Lawrence
Engel)
6-7 Inverness Mews
London W2 3JQ
Tel: 020 7792 4455

Music accountants

O J Kilkenny
6 Lansdowne Mews
London W11 3BH
Tel: 020 7792 9494

Martin Greene
Ravden
55 Loudoun Road
London NW8 0DL
Tel: 020 7625 4545

Sedley Richard
Laurence Voulters
23 Bridford Mews
Devonshire Street
London W1N 1LQ
020 7255 3525

Publications

Billboard
23 Ridgemount Street
London WC1E 7AH
Tel: 020 7323 6686

The Face
Exmouth House
Pine Street
London EC1R 0JL

Future Publishing
(Including Guitarist, Bassist, Total
Guitar, etc.)
30 Monmouth Street
Bath BA1 2BW
Tel: 01225 442244

Kerrang! (also Q and Mojo)
EMAP Metro
Mappin House
4 Winsley House
London W1R 7AR
Tel: 020 7436 1515

NME and Melody Maker
IPC Specialist Group
25th Floor
Kings Reach Tower
Stamford Street
London SE1 9LS
Tel: 020 7251 6229

Time Out
251 Tottenham Court Rd
London W1A 0AB
Tel: 020 7813 3000

The Voice
1st Floor
New Vox House
370 Coldharbour Lane
London SW9 8PL

Professional bodies

Association of Professional
Recording Services
Windsor Square
Silver Street
Reading
Berkshire
RG1 2TH
Tel: 0118 975 6218

British Phonographic Industry (BPI)
25 Savile Row
London W1X 1AA
Tel: 020 72874422

Composers Guild of Great Britain
34 Hanway Street
London W1P 9DE
Tel: 020 7436 0007

Mechanical Copyright Protection
Society (MCPS)
41 Streatham High Road
London SW16 1ER

Musicians Union
60-62 Clapham Rd
London SW9 0JJ
Tel: 020 7582 5566

Performing Right Society (PRS)
20-33 Berners St
London WC1P 4AA
Tel: 020 7580 5544

Phonographic Performance Ltd
(PPL)
Ganton House
14-22 Ganton Street
London W1V 1LB
Tel: 020 7437 0311

Index

Serious about music?

Fast Guide to Cubase VST

Simon Millward

352 pp • 244 x 172 mm • ISBN 1870775 57 0

★ For PC and Mac versions
★ Installation and setting up
★ MIDI and audio features of Cubase VST
★ Hands on projects
★ Steinberg and third party plug-ins
★ Time saving short cuts

£21.95 inc P&P

The Fast Guide to Cubase VST provides the essential information for quickly getting into Steinberg's Cubase VST MIDI sequencing and audio recording package. The book covers all the important aspects of the program including audio and MIDI recording and 'virtual studio technology'.

Installation and setting up of the program are explained, and detailed information on how to record, edit, process and mix digital audio and how to use EQ and effects are all featured. A number of Steinberg and third party plug-in's are explored, and the book shows how to get the best from processing techniques such as compression, gating and limiting. The software is also tested with a range of PC audio cards.

Projects and tutorials throughout the book describe Cubase VST in a number of recording and processing roles, providing valuable insights into how best to use the program for specific tasks.

The Fast Guide to Cubase VST is the ideal companion for all users of the software, from the home sound recordist / musician to the audio professional.

Press reviews

'Projects and tutorials describe valuable insights into how best to use Cubase VST for specific tasks, with plenty of time saving shortcuts' Sound on Sound – Nov 1998
'Great ... background information and walkthrough tutorial features on almost every feature ... a lot more help than the manual and sheds light on bits of Cubase you never knew existed' Future Music – Jan 1999
'A real knowledge base for any user ... the audio side is excellent ... well worth the investment' Basique – Club Cubase magazine

PC Publishing

Export House, 130 Vale Road, Tonbridge, Kent TN9 1SP, UK
Tel 01732 770893 • Fax 01732 770268 • e-mail info@pc-publishing.co.uk
Website http://www.pc-publishing.co.uk

Fast Guide to Emagic Logic

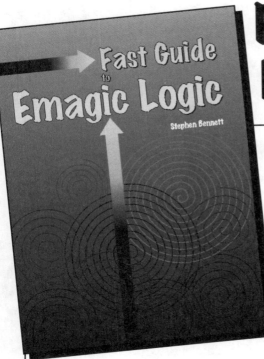

Stephen Bennett

240 pp • 244 x 172 mm
ISBN 1870775 55 4

£16.95 inc P&P

★ For Atari, Macintosh and PC
★ Setting up the program
★ Achieve more musical results
★ User tips and tricks
★ Answers to commonly asked questions
★ Reference for most used functions

Making music is the raison d'etre of Emagic Logic, and this book helps you do just that. Logic is a completely flexible, totally user programmable, object orientated program and can be set up in many ways. This has led to its 'difficult' reputation, and It can appear daunting to the beginner, as well as to the more experienced user migrating from a more traditional sequencing package.

This book takes both types of user from the setting up of the program on Atari, Macintosh and PC platforms, right through to using Logic to make music.

This book describes Logic set-ups that will be useful to a typical user, while introducing some of Logic's more esoteric functions. It also serves as a handy reference to some of Logic's most used functions and contains some tips and tricks to help you with your music making.

Contents: Getting started with Logic, Using Logic, The Score editor, The Environment, The Arrange page, The Event list editor, The Matrix editor, The Transport bar, The Hyper editor, Key commands, Other useful Logic information, Logic menus, Preferences and song settings, Glossary, Logic and the Internet, Index

PC Publishing

Export House, 130 Vale Road, Tonbridge, Kent TN9 1SP, UK
Tel 01732 770893 • Fax 01732 770268 • e-mail info@pc-publishing.co.uk
Website http://www.pc-publishing.co.uk

Making music with digital audio

Direct to disk recording on the PC

Ian Waugh

£16.95 inc P&P

244 x 172 mm * 256 pp
ISBN 1870775 51 1

☆ How to assess your requirements
☆ How to cut through the tech spec jargon
☆ What hardware you 'really' need
☆ How to back up your digital data
☆ How to troubleshoot effectively

The future is digital. Computers have revolutionised the recording and music-making business. Digital audio gives you more flexibility, higher quality and more creative power than multi-track tape recorders. This leading-edge technology is available now to all PC users – and it need not cost the earth.

In this practical and clearly-written book, Ian Waugh explains all aspects of the subject from digital audio basics to putting together a system to suit your own music requirements.

Using the minimum of technical language, the book explains exactly what you need to know about:

☆ Sound and digital audio
☆ Basic digital recording principles
☆ Sample rates and resolutions
☆ Consumer sound cards and dedicated digital audio cards

On a practical level you will learn about, sample editing, digital multi-tracking, digital FX processing, integrating MIDI and digital audio, using sample CDs, mastering to DAT and direct to CD, digital audio and Multimedia

This book is for every musician who wants to be a part of the most important development in music since the invention of the gramophone. It's affordable, it's flexible, it's powerful and it's here now! It's digital and it's the future of music making.

PC Publishing

Export House, 130 Vale Road, Tonbridge, Kent TN9 ISP, UK
Tel 01732 770893 • Fax 01732 770268 • e-mail info@pc-publishing.co.uk
Website http://www.pc-publishing.co.uk

Music on the Internet

Ian Waugh

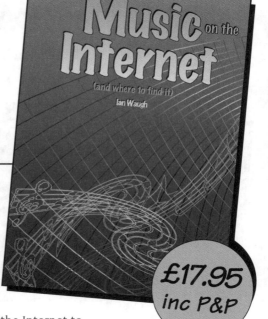

256 pp • 244 x 172 mm • ISBN 1870775 58 9

£17.95 inc P&P

The Internet is the largest music store, encyclopedia and software library in the world. In fact, it is the world! For musicians it's a treasure trove packed with information, news, software, sounds and music files. Through it you can contact the most knowledgeable people in the music business ... if you know where to look. In this practical, easy-to-read and information-packed book, Ian Waugh shows musicians exactly where to look and demonstrates how they can use the Internet to:

★ Get free music software and commercial demos
★ Get updates for their existing software
★ Find out about new products weeks before details appear in the press
★ Get help from manufacturers, developers and fellow musicians

In clear, jargon-free terms it explains:

★ All about the World Wide Web
★ About Web browsers
★ All about Web addresses – URLs
★ How to use Newsgroups and Mailing lists
★ How to Power Search the Web like a pro
★ The importance of high speed Net connections
★ Which modem you really need
★ How to download software

The book also contains the Web addresses of over 700 sites so you can find what you want quickly and without delay. These include music information, on-line magazines, music hardware manufacturers, music software developers, shareware, sound files, music retailers, music publishers, record companies, copyright information, music organisations, sites about composition, artists and user groups.

If you're already on-line, this book will show you how to make the most of your Internet access. If you're not on-line – it will show why you ought to be!

PC Publishing

Export House, 130 Vale Road, Tonbridge, Kent TN9 1SP, UK
Tel 01732 770893 • Fax 01732 770268 • e-mail info@pc-publishing.co.uk
Website http://www.pc-publishing.co.uk